BURPEE

AMERICAN GARDENING SERIES

WATERWISE GARDENING

Lauren Springer

PRENTICE HALL GARDENING

New York ◆ *London* ◆ *Toronto* ◆ *Sydney* ◆ *Tokyo* ◆ *Singapore*

For Michael, my adaptable husband
and for Daphne, my favorite little flower.

Thanks to Rob Proctor, Panayoti and Gwen Kelaidis, Ray Daugherty, Kelly Grummons, Tom Peace, Angela Overy, Mary Ann Heacock and Jim Knopf—a great group of plantspeople dedicated to changing the way America gardens. Their knowledge, generosity and friendship have made this book possible.

PRENTICE HALL GENERAL REFERENCE
15 Columbus Circle
New York, New York, 10023

Library of Congress Cataloging-in-Publication Data

Springer, Lauren.
    Waterwise gardening / Lauren Springer.
        p.   cm.—(Burpee American gardening series)
    Includes index.
    ISBN 0-671-79929-0
    1. Xeriscaping.   2. Drought-tolerant plants.   I. Title.
    II. Series
    SB475.83.S68   1994
    635.9'5—dc20   93-12194
                                                    CIP

Manufactured in the United States of America

First Edition

10   9   8   7   6   5   4   3   2   1

PHOTO CREDITS
Bales, Suzanne F.: pp. 74 bottom, 86 top; **Cresson, Charles O.**: pg. 72 bottom; **Dirr, Michael**: pp. 52 both, 53 middle and bottom, 55 bottom, 56 top, 59 top, 60 top, 64 bottom, 65 both; **Mann, Charles**: pp. 51 both, 53 top, 54, 55, top, 65 middle, 69, 70 both, 71; **Ogden, Scott**: p. 55 middle; **Rollinger, Alan**: p. 59 bottom; **Trager, John**: pg. 73 bottom; **W. Atlee Burpee & Co.**: pp. 34, 86 middle, 87 top; **Woodyard, Cynthia**: pg. 74 top

Illustration of garden plan on page 15 by Elayne Sears
Illustrations on pages 92–94 by Michael Gale

On the cover: In the author's Colorado garden, shrubs, perennials, annuals and succulents grow in rich and vibrant profusion on less than half the water a typical lawn requires.

Preceding page: Well-prepared soil allows Helen Dillon's tour-de-force border in Dublin, Ireland, to thrive on less water.

CONTENTS

INTRODUCTION

As children, the first thing we often learn about plants is that they need water. Many of us began our lifelong passion for gardening clutching a watering can, sprinkling a tomato plant, a sunflower or the family philodendron. Perhaps we watched in amazement as an avocado, potato or a piece of wandering Jew grew roots and sprouted when stuck in a simple glass of water.

Until recently, plentiful water for gardening was a given, even in many of the drier parts of the North American continent. Over the past three decades, water has become an increasingly precious and unreliable commodity.

While this may seem like bad news, in the garden it needn't be. You may already be acquainted with the idea of waterwise gardening. Perhaps you've heard or seen the word *xeriscape*. This term, often misspelled and mispronounced, is derived from the Greek *xeros*, and means dry landscape. Along with the term, a group of steps were developed to simplify and systematize the concepts. This has helped spread the word about waterwise gardening, but the basic concept of gardening with less water is not necessarily limited to those definitions and steps.

Waterwise gardening is just plain old common sense. Good gardening practice means adapting to the conditions at hand. Why have a garden that depends on large amounts of a resource that appears to be ever more expensive and elusive? Why not bank on the future and create a less needy garden? Even if there has always been enough water in your area, a drought-tolerant garden allows you to go away without cumbersome arrangements for watering in absentia. A garden in harmony with its surroundings, both in appearance and in terms of cultural needs, is a healthier, more beautiful garden. Plants that receive the conditions they prefer are better able to fight off pests and diseases. Plants that get by on less water demand less to look their best.

You may want to modify a preexisting garden or start entirely from scratch. Either way, by committing yourself to a waterwise garden you can save money on water and time on unnecessary maintenance, and create an easily cared-for, ecologically sound, attractive garden.

A number of misconceptions exist about waterwise gardening. Dry, barren visions of stone mulch with a few lonely cacti interspersed throughout and perhaps a wagon wheel or cow skull come to mind. While you may have seen such landscapes, they most certainly are not examples of waterwise gardening. They do save on water, but gardens they are not.

Another erroneous belief is that to save water, the gardener must turn his or her back on all the old favorite plants and any that are not "native." Nothing could be further from the truth. Certainly a large portion of the ever-expanding palette of drought-tolerant plants suitable for gardens is native to the North American continent, but to exclude such venerable, tried and true, water-thrifty garden favorites such as lilac, bearded iris, peony or hollyhock just for their foreign pedigree is not only botanical bigotry but horticultural nonsense. Good gardens are democratic. If a plant is attractive, well-adapted and not overly aggressive or invasive, it deserves a place in our gardens.

The other misconception commonly associated with water-conserving gardening is that we are somehow severely limiting ourselves. Having less of something makes us feel cheated. Many of us enjoy watering because it makes us feel we are doing something good for our plants. This isn't always the case. As many, of not more, plants are killed by overwatering as have succumbed to underwatering. It's time to turn our nurturing instincts elsewhere. Waterwise gardening allows us to stop being slaves to the hose, to the water company, to the vagaries of the weather. By creating a garden full of beautiful plants that thrive on less water, we are not limited—we are freed.

This richly textured composition of western native plants needs only 10 inches of water per year.

THE WATERWISE GARDEN PLANNER

A waterwise garden can be whatever you want. Spend some time looking around, and ask yourself some questions before you dive in. What kind of garden appeals to you? Consider styles: formal or informal, romantically loose or serenely restrained. Do you see a garden as a place for tranquil reflection and solitude, as a backdrop to entertaining, or is its raison d'être simply the joy of gardening? Perhaps you want various parts of the garden to perform each of these different roles or others.

Does the existing landscape speak to you and inspire a certain type of garden—a prairie, a rock outcrop, a cliff, for example? Think about how your choice of style fits in with the looks of your property. Also consider the greater surroundings. You may be comfortable with the idea of strongly diverging from the prevailing landscape of the neighborhood, or you may not want to rock the boat and draw that much attention. Let other gardens you admire and the natural landscapes of your region inspire you. What are the dominant colors of the wild plants, the rocks, the soil, the sky? Is the light strong or soft? Is the lay of the land serene and horizontal, such as the fields of the Midwest, the grasslands of the Great Plains, the surface of nearby lakes or the sand and ocean of a calm beachfront? Or does the natural landscape have the drama of cliffs, mesas, a churning surf or mountain vistas? An appreciation for your natural surroundings will help you create a more satisfying garden.

A garden is as personal an expression as the interior of your house and the clothes you wear. Don't let anyone tell you what your garden should or should not look like. Be aware, however, that you may have certain neighborhood covenants or town ordinances that limit your self-expression in the garden; find out what they are before forging ahead, unless you are willing to take on a fight. Innovative gardens, especially prairie gardens, have come up against many archaic town ordinances that require lawns, restrict plant heights and don't allow so-called weeds. More and more, gardeners are winning their battle to make unusual garden styles accepted, but often the fight not only makes enemies out of neighbors but actually takes the gardener to court. If it looks like there might be trouble and you're not up to the fight, express your more adventurous waterwise ideas in a less visible part of your property, such as a fenced or hedge-enclosed backyard rather than the front. By all means find out what you are up against before you run headlong into a big, dramatic departure from the predominant garden style of your area so that you are aware and prepared.

I was not prepared. When I moved to a small town on the semiarid plains in northern Colorado, it never occurred to me that my new garden would create an uproar. My husband and I were attracted by the same qualities that later seemed the root of our conflicts: the town we chose is traditional, close-knit, old-fashioned, clean

In the author's Colorado garden, waterwise plants such as poppies, penstemons and sage create a full look with little water.

and tidy. People take evening and Sunday strolls, sit on front porches, chat daily at the communal mailboxes on each block. The town's pristine appearance is a result of the pride people take in their homes and property. The pretty clapboard homes and picket fences behind the large old elm, ash and silver maple trees that line the streets are kept freshly painted. Lawns are green, weed-free and mown; hedges are neatly trimmed.

The first autumn, when I tore out the Kentucky bluegrass lawn in the front yard and dug it under, I was met with curiosity and perplexed looks. Cars slowed to a crawl as they passed; small crowds of passersby lingered on nice days. "You need to resod?" was the most common question. Things quieted down for the winter as people retreated inside. Come spring, I filled the bare yard with hundreds of plants. Several ornamental grasses grace the plantings, but no lawn.

Suddenly I was met by odd looks from neighbors on their porches whenever I worked outside. Whispers, stares and silence greeted me when I would go get the mail. Morning joggers would make a beeline around to the other side of the street when they approached the garden as if some unseen danger lurked among the jumble of plants. Some people actually threw litter from their car windows and brought their dogs to our property. I was ready to pack up and leave.

After that first season, things began to change. As the garden filled in, growing more lush and colorful each season, I sensed a slow but steady change in the tide of antipathy I had felt at first. Old-timers would point out plants from the mountains and plains they recognized, or spot an old-fashioned flower they remembered from their mothers' or grandparents' gardens. Kids passing by on their way to school would stop to watch the butterflies, bees and other insects, or pet the fuzzy lamb's ear leaves. Parents would bring their babies and toddlers by for a look; people began to ask for seeds and starts.

Now, several years later, we have converted most doubters. A few die-hard detractors still find the garden offensive, "a wild patch of weeds," but the uproar has died down. Some people prefer other styles, but few actually dislike my garden anymore. More water-wise flower gardens are pushing their way into lawn territory each season. Was it worth it? You bet.

GARDEN STYLES

The great thing about waterwise gardens is that you can tailor them to suit any style. Perhaps you want to echo the serene look of a well-designed traditional suburban landscape, where green is the dominant color, cool and refreshing. You may also appreciate the idea of low maintenance. Trees give shade and privacy; shrubs and groundcovers add variety of color, texture and form, and a fresh wave of green turf weaves the whole picture together harmoniously and gracefully. By planting a more drought-resistant turf grass, replacing difficult areas of lawn such as on slopes, in thin strips and overly shaded areas under trees with attractive mulches and easy-care waterwise groundcovers and shrubs, you can create the same look and have a much less time- and water-consuming landscape.

Alternatively, you may want the garden to be an extension of your home, an outdoor living space or garden room of sorts. The nonliving elements of the house that reach out to the garden—walls, doors, windows, porches, patios—can be integrated into the garden by repeating their colors in your choice of plants. By echoing the color and texture of the materials of your home in contain-

These street strips were transformed into a riot of color that needs no supplementary irrigation.

ers, fences, furniture and statuary that go in the garden, the transition from indoors to out is more pleasing. Both a formal garden style and the so-called Mediterranean garden take much from this approach.

The Formal Garden

At the root of formal design is a sense of predictable structure. This can be reflected in the choice of plants—the polished look of some glossy evergreen foliages, the manicured, carpetlike effect of evenly growing groundcovers, symmetry in the habit of certain trees and shrubs or the tall, stately, vertical flower spikes of some perennials. Pruning, shearing and mowing plants, molding them as living sculpture, creates a controlled appearance, adding formality to the line, shape and surface of plants. Often formality in a landscape integrates the house both visually and functionally with the garden. Clipped hedges form outdoor walls or boundaries. Symmetry of a planting mirrors the symmetry of, say, a doorway or facade.

You can also express formality by your placement of plants. Repeat the same species of plant at regular intervals; stagger heights in a planned pattern; group plants together that share a restricted color palette. A garden grows more formal as it becomes increasingly obvious that the gardener, not just nature, has a hand in where, how and which plants are growing there. Traditonally, formal gardens are often filled with plants not known for their

water thrift. The truth is, any formal garden can be made more waterwise by choosing plants that require less water.

The Mediterranean Garden

This style transforms a garden into a beckoning outdoor room. It was born in a region where the climate supports outdoor living much of the year. A Mediterranean garden works well in small spaces and for those of us who spend a lot of time outdoors doing things others might do indoors—eating, entertaining, reading and just plain relaxing. Usually part of this garden incorporates a floor of stone or brick; often a change of levels divides the garden, adding interest and separating areas for different activities. Walls, made both of plants and of hard materials, further give a sense of garden space as an extension of the house. Plants are allowed to spill over and from within walls of stone, brick or adobe, softening and unifying the design. Vines and other woody plants are often trained on these vertical surfaces as well as on trellises and arbors to create light shade from hot midday and afternoon sun. Ornaments—statues and well-planted containers—decorate the outdoor "rooms." The typical palette of plants favors small plants that invite close scrutiny—plants with intricate textures and aromatic flowers or foliage. Traditionally, attractive herbs such as thyme, rosemary and lavender are included

alongside sun-loving perennials, shrubs and perhaps a small tree or two. Containers provide a place to highlight plants that need extra care and water—carefully trimmed miniature topiary, roses trained as standards or fragrant gardenia bushes, for example.

Because heat and drought are an integral part of the Mediterranean climate, garden-worthy plants native to that area are suited to many other water-wise garden styles as well. That same heat and drought invite the lovely counterpoint of a small-scale water feature, such as a small pool or

The simple, clean lines of this formal planting come alive in autumn as the fiery scarlet foliage of dwarf plumbago contrasts with dwarf privet and santolina.

This elegant container features euphorbia and variegated Helichrysum petiolatum, two water-thrifty choices for easy care.

fountain, among the sun-loving plants. This pleasing combination often finds a home in the Mediterranean garden style.

The delightful sight, sound and feel of water, so refreshing and desirable when heat and drought dominate, are easily

Pale variegated thyme and lacy blue rue create a fine herbal tapestry.

integrated into a waterwise garden without being incongruous—when done on a modest scale. You may think filling a small pond or pool with gallons of water is wasteful, yet next to an entire landscape that is irrigated inefficiently and is filled with water-greedy plants, it compares most favorably. Plant your water feature with water-lilies and other aquatic plants for interest and to cut down on surface evaporation. Even if you leave it free of plants, whether to swim in or just as a pretty mirrorlike design feature, it will waste a lot less water than the large area typically given over to thirsty lawn. The same is true of a fountain when it is designed to recirculate water. A water-wise garden need not be a waterless garden.

The Herb Garden

Another option for a beautiful water-saving garden is the herb garden. Traditionally this is small in size and formal in layout, often with strongly symmetrical lines. An herb garden is intimate, meant for meandering and lingering, for the smelling, tasting, pinching and picking of its bounty. Often flowering plants that are not necessarily culinary or medicinal are included for their visual appeal, fragrance or for cutting and bringing in the house. Small evergreen shrubs add structure, lining the paths as sheared specimens or trimmed hedges. These may be herbal in nature, such as bay, lavender, germander and lavender cotton, but they need not be. For the truly inspired pruner and shearer, the fanciful artistry of a knot garden is a lovely challenge. Here low-growing herbs or similar plants with attractively colored and textured leaves are planted in intertwining abstract swirls and patterns. Because of the drought-tolerant nature of many herbs, an herb garden makes an excellent waterwise garden style. Consider incorporating more thirsty herbs by growing them in containers laced decoratively within the garden; this way you can more easily tend to their needs without wasting water.

A sunny herb garden invites the onlooker with delightful aromas.

THE ROLE OF THE LAWN

The part of our collective gardening consciousness most resistant to change involves the thirsty lawn. We grew up with it, we are comfortable with it, we expect it. It seems hard to come up with alternatives when there are so few yet put to practice to serve as models. There are many different approaches: the most conservative, which in essence keeps the lawn as is; the more moderate, which keeps the look but changes the plants; and the most aggressive approach, which finds true lawn alternatives, in terms of both design and plants.

A few simple modifications in watering practices and a slight down-sizing of your lawn will help make an existing traditional garden conserve water. A step beyond more efficient turf irrigation and maintenance entails replacing the lawn with mulches and drought-tolerant groundcovers in areas where it serves no function. Water savings increase even more dramatically when you plant a water-conserving species of turf grass. Some of these grasses, such as buffalo and zoysia grass, are brown later into the growing season than the thirstier cool-season grasses that typically make up a lawn. One way of overcoming the doldrums of a dormant lawn in early spring is to interplant small bulbs such as crocus, snow iris and species tulips. These water-thrifty bulbs are tough enough to grow through the grass, and their foliage is sparse and fine, not much of a detraction when it "ripens," as it must, in late spring and early summer. As the lawn begins to green up and grow taller, the fading bulb foliage sinks down into it; by early summer it can be raked away or mowed down. Bunchgrasses and grasses with above-ground stolons, such as buffalo grass, are best for interplanting bulbs and are preferable to the overly competitive underground rhizomes of Bermuda or thirsty Kentucky bluegrass. However, bulbs can even be naturalized in such a grass if planted where it is thinner and weaker, such as under the shade of a deciduous tree. Crocuses, winter aconites, squills and small daffodils all do well in thin Kentucky bluegrass. The bulbs and soil are warmed by the early spring sun through the tree's bare branches, and are kept cool by the shade of the tree's expanded foliage during the hot summer months.

Be generous when planting diminutive bulbs, for they make an impact only in large numbers—think about naturalistic sweeps in the hundreds, not a handful here and there. They are not expensive. You can plant bulbs in an already established lawn, but it is much less of a battle if you do it the same season you plant the lawn, before the grass has thickened into a turf and the root system has grown dense. Water the area before you plant to soften the soil, and use a bulb dibble, a tool that pokes small holes in the soil the size of the bulbs. If you have a hard, heavy soil, you can attach

WATERWISE PLANTS FOR THE HERB GARDEN

*Absinthe**	*Jojoba*
Aloe vera	*Lavender**
*Anise**	*Lavender cotton**
*Bayberry**	*Marjoram**
Borage	*Mormon tea*
*Caraway**	*Mullein*
*Carob**	*Nasturtium**
*Catmint**	*Oregano**
*Catnip**	*Pomegranate*
*Chamomile**	*Poppy seed*
Chicory	*Pot marigold**
*Chives**	*Pyrethrum**
*Coriander**	*Rosemary**
*Cumin**	*Rue**
*Curry**	*Safflower*
*Dill**	*Saffron*
*Egyptian onion**	*Sage**
*Eucalyptus**	*Scented geranium**
*Fennel**	*Senna*
*Garlic**	*Tansy**
*Germander**	*Tarragon**
Hops	*Thyme**
Horehound	*Winter savory**
*Horsemint**	*Wormwood**
*Hyssop**	*Yarrow**

*Fragrant

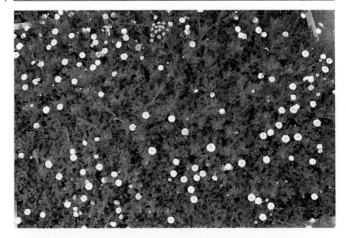

Double-flowered chamomile, a wonderfully fragrant groundcover, requires much less water than most lawns.

In early spring, a still-dormant lawn of drought-tolerant buffalo grass glows with small ruby tulips.

a large 1- or 1½-inch bit to a hand-held power drill to make your holes. (Just don't plan on digging hundreds of little holes with a trowel; you'll probably never finish the job, and if you do, you may be soured on gardening forever.)

Once planted, the bulbs go on to self-sow and divide, their clumps multiplying and thickening with time. Early each year, your lawn will be the star of the entire garden when the tiny, richly hued bulbs open to the warming sunlight, like jewels spangling the tawny, still dormant grass.

WATERWISE BULBOUS PLANTS

Agapanthus (lily of the Nile)
Allium (ornamental onion)*
Amaryllis belladonna (*Brunsvigia rosea*; naked lady)*
Anemone blanda (Grecian windflower)
Asphodeline (Jacob's rod)
Asphodelus (asphodel)
Babiana (baboon flower)*
Bloomeria crocea (golden stars)
Brodiaea/Dichelostemma/Triteleia (blue dicks, wild hyacinth)*
Brunsvigia josephinae (Josephine's lily)
Bulbine
Bulbinella
Calochortus (mariposa lily, sego lily, fairy lantern)
Colchicum (autumn crocus)
Crocosmia/Montbretia/Tritonia
*Crocus**
Dietes vegeta (fortnight lily)
Eremurus (foxtail lily)*
Fritillaria persica
Galtonia (summer hyacinth)*
Gladiolus (not the large hybrids)*
Habranthus (rain lily)
Hermodactylus tuberosus (widow iris)*
Hesperocallis undulata (ajo lily, desert lily)*

*Homeria**
*Iris bucharica**
Iris danfordiae (golden snow iris)*
*Iris histrioides**
Iris reticulata (snow iris)*
Iris unguicularis (winter iris)*
Ixia (corn lily)
Ixiolirion (Tartarian lily)
Lewisia (bitterroot)
Lycoris (surprise lily)
Milla biflora (Mexican star)*
Muscari (grape hyacinth)*
Nectaroscordum
Nemastylis (prairie iris)
Nerine
Nothoscordum (grace garlic)
Ornithogalum (chincherinchee, star of Bethlehem)
Pancratium (sea daffodil)*
Pardanthopsis (vesper iris)*
Romulea (African crocus)
Sparaxis/Streptanthera (wand flower)
Spiloxene
Sternbergia (autumn daffodil)*
Tulbaghia (society garlic)*
*Tulipa**
Urginea maritima (sea onion)
Watsonia (bugle lily)
Zephyranthes (fairy lily—some)
Zigadenus (camas—some)
*Fragrant

The most dramatic way to cut down on your lawn's water-wasting ways is to get rid of it altogether, replacing it with drought-tolerant plants that can take some foot traffic, and non-living materials for paths and an entertaining area, if one is wanted. One way to do this in a small garden is to plant the perimeter with shrubs, working in toward the center—the patio. Groundcovers, easy-care perennials and bulbs weave between the shrubs. Showy plants that need more primping and water spill from containers along the edge of the patio, softening its edges and making the transition from the more natural to the manicured. A gentle, pleasing transition is made from the house to the patio and the garden. The garden is at once a showcase for plants and a beckoning outdoor retreat, all without a lawn.

A SMALL BACKYARD OASIS

I designed this garden for a small, rectangular backyard, 50 feet long and 30 feet wide. Waterwise, low-maintenance plants have been selected, easily obtainable and with a wide range of climatic adaptability. A long season of bloom, attractive foliage and pleasant fragrance are all emphasized. The cost of the plants at retail price (not including installation) should fall well below $2,000.

TREES

1 _Cercis occidentalis_ or _C. canadensis_ v. _mexicana_ (redbud)
2 _Juniperus virginiana_ cv. or _J. scopulorum_ cv. (columnar juniper)
3 _Koelreuteria paniculata_ (goldenrain tree)

SHRUBS

4 _Cotinus coggygria_ 'Royal Purple' (purple smokebush)
5 _Cytisus_ × 'Moonlight' (Scottish broom)
6 _Hibiscus syriacus_ 'Bluebird' (rose of Sharon)
7 _Syringa laciniata_ (cutleaf lilac)
8 _Syringa_ × _persica_ (Persian lilac)

ROSES

9 _Rosa rugosa_ 'Alba'
10 _Rosa rugosa_ 'Jens Munk'
11 _Rosa spinosissima_ 'Frühlingsgold'

PERENNIALS
ACCENT PLANTS

12 _Crambe cordifolia_ (giant sea kale)
13 _Iris_ × _germanica_ 'Beverly Sills'

14 _Lavatera thuringiaca_ 'Barnsley' (shrubby lavatera)
15 _Yucca filamentosa_

MIXERS AND FILLERS

16 _Coreopsis_ × 'Moonbeam' (tickseed)
17 _Limonium latifolium_ (sea lavender)
18 _Linum perenne_ (blue flax)
19 _Oenothera macrocarpa_ (Ozark sundrop)
20 _Perovskia_ (Russian sage)

BULBS

21 _Crocus_
22 _Iris reticulata_ (snow iris)
23 _Lycoris squamigera_ (surprise lily)
24 _Tulipa_ Darwin hybrids (tulip)

GROUNDCOVERS AND EDGINGS

25 _Brunnera macrophylla_ (Siberian forget-me-not)
26 _Callirhoe involucrata_ (poppy mallow)
27 _Campanula poscharskyana_ (creeping bellflower)
28 _Cerastium tomentosum_ (snow-in-summer)
29 _Geranium sanguineum_ v. _striatum_ (Lancaster cranesbill)
30 _Hemerocallis_ 'Hyperion' (daylily)
31 _Juniperus horizontalis_ cv. (low blue juniper)
32 _Oenothera speciosa_ (Mexican evening primrose)
33 _Stachys byzantina_ 'Silver Carpet' (lamb's ear)

This low-maintenance planting with a pastel scheme uses plants adapted to most regions.

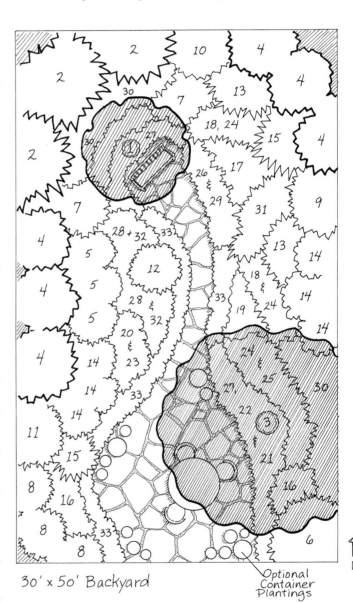

30' x 50' Backyard

Optional Container Plantings

FLAGSTONE FILLERS

Antennaria parvifolia (pussytoes)
Thymus pseudolanuginosus (woolly thyme)

THE HILLSIDE GARDEN

A number of waterwise garden styles take their inspiration from the natural landscape. Examples are as diverse as rock, cliff, desert and prairie gardens. Many of us live in the city or suburbs and yearn for the untamed beauty of the wilderness. These styles allow us to bring a little bit of that into our front- or backyard.

Hillside and cliff gardens are ideally suited for water conservation; because of their slope, they require plants that can take sharp drainage. It is difficult to water a steep slope well and can actually be downright dangerous, due to erosion and the potential for slippage. If the slope faces south or west without shade, the heat will make it absolutely necessary to grow truly drought- and heat-tolerant plants.

Transforming an existing hillside or cliff into a garden usually has wonderful results. The vertical aspect adds a dramatic dimension, showing plants to great advantage at or above eye level. Cascading, trailing and draping plant forms look especially good. Often a steep, natural slope appears harsh before it is planted, whether it be raw, exposed soil or extensive rock outcrops.

Plants soften the nonliving landscape. On the practical side, plants also help stabilize the slope by binding soil and stone with their roots. You can create a pleasing area by building "steps" into a slope, held in place by stone, brick, rot-resistant wood or some other hardscape material. These steps also make it much easier to work in the garden. This practice is called terracing, and has been used in agriculture for many centuries in hilly and mountainous regions throughout the world. It works equally well for ornamental hillside gardens.

THE ROCK GARDEN

Rock gardens take the harmonious marriage of the living and nonliving elements of the landscape one step further. Plant and rock become allies, evoking the beauty of the

At Denver Botanic Gardens, a hot, dry hillside becomes an oasis of color when planted with verbena, sagebrush, native grasses and golden chamisa.

world's mountainous regions. Stone plays a unifying theme in the garden, weaving its color and texture throughout. During times of the year when the plants are not particularly showy, these same rocks take on a strong design role, adding interest with their shape and placement. The stones also act as a mulch, conserving water, cooling the roots of the plants and keeping out competitive weeds. A rock creates microclimates, sheltering a nearby plant from wind and frost, cooling a small nook in its shadow while warming the area near its sun-baked side. The truly avid rock gardener joins art with science, using these microclimates to grow a huge variety of plants in a beautiful setting.

Rock gardens can make ideal waterwise gardens. Traditionally, a rock garden's plant palette harks from the mountainous regions of the world, for that is what the style was originally meant to replicate. Generally these plants are small in stature, often with attractive bun or cushionlike forms and evergreen foliage. The majority are adapted to the rigors of high alpine life—fierce wind, strong sunlight, steep, rocky, rapidly draining soil and severe cold. There is no reason, however, to limit yourself to mountain plants. Many water-wise plants—Mediterranean, desert and steppe natives, for example—look very much at home and thrive in rock gardens. A graceful rock garden is easiest to create if your existing landscape already includes stone formations, but most rock gardens are built from scratch, rock and all. Choose rock that is either local or blends well with the colors of your surroundings. Don't mix many different types of rock; it gives the garden a haphazard, disjointed look. Larger boulders or slabs, while difficult and expensive to install, usually look better than small rocks. To give the garden a more natural feel and to avoid the awful look of a moonscape or rock slide, only one-third to one-half of each rock should be visible. A rock garden can be as large a project as you wish, but due to the smaller size of the plants and their often intricate forms and textures, it is a waterwise style ideally suited to limited space.

Quite to the contrary, both prairie and desert gardens look to expansive, open, natural landscapes for inspiration. While its individual plant components may vary, the prairie or meadow garden is quite a precise, defined garden expression. Such a garden is not made by sprinkling the contents of a "meadow in a can" casually over an area, or rolling out an expensive piece of so-called wildflower sod, though. These may produce pretty, but short-lived, plantings. In a true prairie garden, specific grasses and wildflowers grow densely together in long-lasting harmony.

In this spring rock garden scene, the unusual beauty Iris bucharica *joins pretty waterwise commoners basket-of-gold and purple rock cress.*

PRAIRIE GARDENS

Prairie gardens have no trees and few, if any, shrubs, and depend on full sunlight for success. While not highly dramatic or bold, prairie gardens capture the essence of wildness. They are a series of wonderful contradictions—at once serene and vibrant, predictable yet ever changing. They tend to make use of native plants more than other garden styles, for they attempt to recreate a specific wild landscape with its unique plant community and ecosystem. Along with these plants comes a dividend: the rich and diverse animal world they attract. Your prairie garden stirs with the sudden, manic dart of a thrush, the lazy flutter of butterflies. Prairie gardens have been compared to the sea; at a glance, they appear calm and almost monotonous, but a closer look reveals a complex world of natural rhythms, in the movement of the wind through the grasses, the buzz and hum of the insects, the song of the birds, the rustling of wildlife and the changing colors of the seasonal flowers.

All but those prairie gardens seeking to recreate a moist meadow can be considered waterwise, for the natural models—the tallgrass, midgrass and the shortgrass prairies of North America—are acclimated to drought, the first and second seasonally, the last almost year 'round. You will need to water regularly the first season to get the plants established, as is true of any other waterwise garden.

At the heart of a prairie garden is a well-prepared soil rich in organic matter, an approximation of what the prairie has created for itself for eons, and its constituent plants expect no

Perennials and bulbs brighten Gordon Koon's Colorado rock garden, a lovely water-saving solution for a difficult slope.

Indian paintbrush, coneflower and gaillardia float in a sea of blue grama grass in this drought-tolerant prairie garden.

Drought-loving annuals desert bluebell, Dahlberg daisy and white portulaca spill onto a hot pavement.

less. One or more native bunchgrasses or thinly spreading grasses form the dominant backdrop through which any number of wildflowers, mainly perennial, grow. Choose grasses and perennials well-suited to your climate. Purist prairie gardens recreate a particular combination of plants that actually occurs in the wild; you needn't be that exacting.

Some successful prairie or meadow gardens incorporate a number of plants not native to this continent at all, but similar in feel. How orthodox you want to be is up to you. You can create a prairie garden with small plants or by sowing seed, which is much cheaper but requires more attention to preliminary weeding and watering. Prairie gardens take some work and vigilance the first year or two, good soil preparation and careful weeding being essential to a good start. If you are redoing an area that was planted in turf, kill off the grass with glyphosate and plant through the dead sod; it will serve as a weed-suppressing and moisture-conserving mulch and a source of organic matter.

A prairie planting becomes more self-reliant with time. The tough grasses and perennials crowd out weeds and need little water once established. The natural look of the style is en-hanced by leaving spent flowers to form seeds and seedheads, which feed wildlife and go on to grow into more plants. Mowing is not absolutely necessary, but in nature the prairie was grazed by buffalo and other herbivores, so in their absence most prairie gardeners feel it is good to do at least one rough cutting during the dormant season to help the flowers compete with the grasses, remove debris and make room and air for germinating seedlings and new growth. Controlled fires can also be used, invigorating a tired planting, clearing thatch and weeds and helping dormant seeds germinate, but these require more knowledge and experience. Be sure to check with local authorities before attempting a burn. Well-established prairie gardens rank perhaps as the most low-maintenance waterwise style of all, along with desert gardens.

DESERT GARDENS

A froth of dryland wildflowers softens the stark spikes of yuccas in this casual desert garden.

A desert garden, like a prairie garden, evokes a specific natural setting. Obviously, the scene is adapted to a scarcity of water. Unlike the prairie garden, here the plants are widely spaced, as they are in the desert. The individual plants have importance. With their dramatic shapes, many desert plants are perfect for the role of living sculpture. Grouped naturalistically, set next to boulders or arranged in small clusters rather than dotted haphazardly across the landscape, the plants create rhythmic patterns that form a harmonious whole. The color and texture of the soil between the plants unifies the composition, much as a lawn does in a "traditional" landscape, or as stone does in a rock garden. Contouring the land by building shallow swales and low berms not only adds dimension to the garden; it also helps control the flow and make use of precious water if it channels moisture toward the plants. Stones are a vital design element in desert gardens, both as focal points and as mulch. A cover of fine gravel conserves moisture, adds unifying color and texture, and helps form a good seedbed for self-sowing desert wildflowers.

Desert gardens lean heavily toward a plant vocabulary of cacti, agaves, aloes, yuccas and other succulents. These plants give the style its architectural character. Still, a garden made up entirely of these lacks softness and spontaneity. The strong, rigid evergreen lines and shapes of these plants left alone by themselves can make the garden seem plastic, unchanging, like a botanical wax museum. By incorporating more ephemeral, delicately textured desert flowers, both annuals and perennials, you recreate the beautiful fleeting flower color that seasonally washes over the desert. Add a few fine-textured, highly drought-tolerant shrubs and trees such as creosote bush, ephedra, mesquite or palo verde to contrast with the stiffer plants, and the whole picture is softened.

THE COTTAGE GARDEN

A look very different from the desert garden is that of the water-wise cottage garden. What this style lacks in structure and year-'round interest, it makes up for in its infectious celebration of flowers. A tousle of perennials, bulbs and annuals dominates; shrubs and trees play supporting roles. Color is the theme of the cottage garden. This popular style has a long history, and its blowsy profusion seems the antithesis of what some people mistakenly think of as a typical water-wise garden. Surprisingly, that same old-fashioned charm so inextricably entwined with the prototypical moist, lush English cottage garden can be created using very little water. The key lies in choosing the right plants. Make sure to include plants with attractive foliage and varied blooming periods, and when combining them, consider how the shapes and textures—not just the colors—play off one another.

My garden is a waterwise cottage garden. I chose this style for two reasons: it fits best with our old-fashioned clapboard house and picket fence and softens the strong rectangular lines of the lot; and it allows me to grow a larger number of plants in a confined area than any other style (except perhaps a rock garden). My cottage garden gave quick results: Even the first year it was colorful, thanks to an abundance of annuals to fill in the gaps. Now favorite old-fashioned plants such as cosmos, love-in-a-mist, oriental poppies and Father Hugo rose mingle with western American wildflowers and a growing number of new and unusual introductions from other drought-ridden lands. A newcomer to the concept of water-wise gardening would never guess the lush abundance that spills out onto the sidewalks actually uses less than half the water a typical lawn does, or that the colorful far reaches of the property get by on no additional irrigation at all.

Let this handful of garden styles be a starting point to inspire you. Mix different aspects you like, discard elements you don't, and forge boldly ahead in creating a waterwise garden that suits you.

In the author's cottage garden, sunset hues and the fullness of late summer belie the planting's water-thrifty ways.

DESIGNING A WATERWISE GARDEN

Once you have decided to save water, a bewildering number of choices unfold before you. The styles and options put forth in the preceding chapter only nick the surface. Unlimited opportunity is exhilarating, but can also be overwhelming. Where to begin?

Ask yourself some basic questions. Take time to answer these honestly and carefully; then you'll be ready to approach the change to a more water-saving garden without danger of disappointment. Finding parameters and placing limits help turn wishes into reality.

First, do you want to start from scratch? Perhaps you must, if the existing garden is in bad shape or if you have a new homesite. Perhaps you're happy with some aspects of your garden but want to change others—for instance, you wish to keep the trees but replace most of the lawn with shrubs, groundcovers and perennials. Or, you may feel that you like the look of your garden just as it is, but still want to conserve water. By doing just a few things—replacing certain plants with more drought-tolerant species, decreasing the size of the lawn by adding water-thrifty groundcovers and mulch in its place, and making maintenance and watering more efficient—you can have virtually the same garden with less water. Therein lies the beauty of waterwise gardening; it is versatile enough to apply no matter what your plan for your garden, be it a total overhaul or minor conversion.

Next, ask yourself what you are willing and able to do. A waterwise garden can be installed for about the same price as a traditional landscape of similar size and complexity. Remember that a waterwise garden pays for itself over time. While the initial cost of design, plants and installation may be sizeable, your investment is returned through 30 percent to 80 percent water savings and increased property value; a good waterwise landscape is often worth about 15 percent of the total value of your home. At first you may be disheartened by high water usage; all plants, even desert-adapted cacti, need regular irrigation to get established. This will reverse itself soon enough, so be patient. Plants, especially slower-growing shrubs and trees, appreciate in value as they mature. A well-maintained, five-year-old planting is worth 5 percent to 10 percent more than when first installed; a 10-year-old landscape, 10 percent to 20 percent more. To reduce initial cost, consider doing some of the design and installation yourself, and maintain the garden on your own. An ambitious project where ground is moved, slopes created or flattened and hardscape (such as a pool, patio, walls, paths or stones for a rock garden) is installed will probably require the help of professionals for both design and installation. A garden plan heavy on woody plants may require outside help at the outset with planting, but maintenance will be minimal. A garden emphasizing perennials and annuals may require less muscle to plant but entails more ongoing work. How much gardening are you able and willing to do?

Autumn paints a perfect picture at one of the world's finest gardens, Wave Hill, built on a rocky, dry hillside overlooking the Hudson River in the Bronx, New York.

GET TO KNOW YOUR SITE

This tranquil spot is brightened by the luminescent blossoms and silver foliage of white-flowered rose campion, a tough plant for dry shade.

Examine your garden site for possibilities and limitations. A basic understanding of your climate—sun intensity, typical high and low temperatures, humidity—is essential in choosing the best plants for your garden.

Apart from the climate of your particular region, your site will also have microclimates created by wind, sun exposure, hard landscape features and soil type. These also determine what plants will thrive. If the garden is windy, you may want to plant or build a wind screen. A windy garden can be colder than a wind-still one if the prevailing winds are from the north or from across a body of water, or hotter if they come from the south or across land. Wind is not always a bad thing; it can help reduce insect and disease problems, and make your plants grow thickly and compactly. Depending on your climate, a cool wind may be a great boon to you and your plants, or a warm wind may be just what you need.

Sun exposure—the interplay of sun and shade in the garden dependent on the compass direction the garden faces—also affects your garden. A northern exposure, cooler and less sunny, is a welcome site for many plants in hot climates, while in colder and more northerly regions it is not particularly hospitable. The south side can bake unbearably in Texas; in Montana it offers a most congenial place for a garden. Western exposures are generally less desirable for gardening than eastern ones, for they are hot in the afternoon, frying plants in hot climates. In colder regions, this afternoon sun can warm up unprepared plants too soon, breaking their protective dormancy and making them susceptible to frost damage.

Shade, created by the house and other structures on a site as well as by trees and other plants that already exist or are to be added, must be taken into account. Gardeners tend to view shade as an obstacle to be overcome rather than a desirable garden feature. While dense shade from evergreens or tall buildings can host only a few plants, the more generous growing conditions found under most mature trees or in an eastern exposure suit many a plant. Shade can be a valuable ally in helping make your garden more water-conserving. A large number of plants, even many sun lovers, prefer light shade during the hottest months of the year. The cooler temperatures and higher humidity found in shaded areas help reduce water loss. A tree or structure also cuts down on wind, slowing evaporation from nearby plants and from the soil itself. Think carefully before you decide to remove any large, healthy deciduous tree. Not only does such a tree serve the garden well by cooling the air and blocking wind, but you may miss what it does for your outdoor living space as well. A mature tree is often the single most valuable item in a landscape when it comes to selling a property. In most cases you should leave the tree; in fact, many gardens would do well if more trees were planted.

Another important aspect to note is slope. The steeper the slope, the more prone that area is to drought. Water tends to run off a slope rather than penetrate the soil. Once it does reach deep into the soil, it tends to move more rapidly through it on a slope than on a flat area, leaving the top too dry and the foot of the slope too wet. In addition, steep slopes erode easily, and irrigating them may speed up this process. To deal with steep slopes, you can be aggressive and bulldoze them. The down side of such a drastic approach is the expense and the damage you may do to your soil. Heavy machinery compacts soil, and moving large amounts of earth destroys the natural layers of topsoil and subsoil. Alternatives exist. If you are fortunate enough to have natural rock outcrops as part of the slope, consider incorporating these into a naturalistic hillside garden. If not, an attractive option is terracing. Either way, you have helped control erosion, made water absorption more efficient and created a plant-friendly area for a garden.

LAWN AND LAWN ALTERNATIVES

The next step in designing a water-wise garden is to evaluate the lawn. The lawn is more than a traditional feature in our landscapes; it borders on religion. Hours are spent mowing, watering, fertilizing and keeping it free of all interlopers, be they lowly fungus, beetle, dog or cat with a mission, or opportunistic plants known as weeds. Lawn care is as much a part of suburban and small-town family ritual as barbeques and touch football. When I tore out most of our front lawn and replaced it with water-thrifty, colorful shrubs, perennials and annuals, it was almost as if I had hung the American flag upside down. Compared with the majority of American landscapes, where the lawn dominates to the exclusion of most other plants, our garden was certainly unusual and novel, but hardly the equivalent of heresy. The monotony of American landscaping is mainly the fault of overemphasis on the lawn.

Lawns are not a bad thing. They are refreshing to look at, reducing glare near hardscapes. They cool the air around them. In areas prone to brush fire, they protect the house. Best of all, lawns are a delight for barefoot walks, picnics and all kinds of outdoor play. Lawn grasses are ideally suited to foot traffic, withstanding trampling more than any other group of plants. Still, there is no reason lawn should cover every square foot of a property.

The average lawn guzzles 35 inches or more of water per year, three to four times more than any other area in the garden. Several factors contribute to this water greed. A great deal of water is lost to evaporation from the grassy surface, especially in sunny climates with low humidity. The prevailing species of grasses used in lawns tend to require a large amount of water to stay dependably green most of the year. Also, many lawns are installed on lousy soil, typically right after building is complete. The excavated subsoil is spread around by a front-end loader, leveled by a tractor, and then either sown or sodded in grass. The poor turf doesn't have much of a chance to develop a good root system from which to take up water in such abused, compacted soil. Lastly, most irrigation practices are far from efficient. Typical lawn watering results in almost half of the water being wasted. A poor pattern of application causes too much water to be applied in one area and not enough in another, forcing more frequent waterings to make up for the shortfall in the drier areas. Often there is overspray—the watering pattern laps out onto pavement or some surface other than the lawn. Most sprinklers emit too much water too quickly for the lawn to absorb, causing runoff and more waste. Water penetration is further hampered by thatch buildup and quick evaporation. So what little water does make it into the soil doesn't go very deep. This promotes shallow root growth, and the vicious cycle is complete. Shallow roots are more prone to drying out, so more water is needed.

The typical lawn, stressed and inefficient because of all these mistakes, depends on supplementary food and water, and weed, pest and disease controls aside from regular mowing. The excessive fertilizers, weed killers and pesticides applied to lawns have found their way into our groundwater, have gone with runoff into our ponds, lakes and streams, and are linked to health problems in wildlife, pets and people.

For a healthy, attractive, waterwise alternative, try changing some of these misguided practices. But more than that, consider limiting the areas devoted to turf. If you already have a lawn in place, reduce its size, and change its shape to make watering more efficient; squares and rectan-

On her street strips, the author replaced thirsty grass with a jamboree of drought-tolerant plants, both native and exotic.

Waterwise Lawn Grasses and Alternatives

Warm-Season Grasses

Buffalo grass (Buchloe dactyloides): *Native fine-textured sod-former. Most drought-tolerant of all. Muted gray-green color. Does not tolerate shade. Stays low, 4 to 6 inches tall; low-maintenance, can be mowed at 3 inches or left natural. Prefers an alkaline clay but is extremely adaptable. Grows in the North, South, from deserts to San Francisco Bay area. Turns brown in complete drought. No fertilizer needed. Fast-growing,*

forms sod in one season. Get pretreated seed for best germination. Dainty seed heads can be pretty. 'Prairie' is a good, thick selection with no visible seedheads.

Bermuda grass (Cynodon dactylon): *Sod-former, rich green, southern equivalent to Kentucky bluegrass. Fair drought tolerance. The common form is more drought-tolerant than the hybrids. Turns brown with frost. Good choice for the hot climates of the South and Southwest, not good in regions with cold winters. Tolerates*

most soil types and salt. Does not take shade. Vigorous grower, highly invasive, can be weedy where not wanted. Needs some fertilization. Mow to 1 inch. 'NuMex Sahara' is a more drought-tolerant selection.

Blue grama (Bouteloua gracilis): *Native bunchgrass, fine-textured, blue-gray leaves, second most drought-tolerant grass after buffalo grass. Likes alkaline soil. Goes dormant in extended drought, quick to re-green. Intolerant of shade. Not as adaptable as buffalo grass; best in cool, dry climates. No fertilizer necessary. Not as durable underfoot as other grasses listed. Nice seedheads, like eyelashes. Mow to 3 inches or leave natural at 12 to 18 inches. Excellent prairie garden grass.*

Zoysia grass (Zoysia spp.): *Low-growing sod grass, good drought tolerance. Slow-growing, little mowing necessary, to 1 inch. Good in hot climates, not in cool. Likes*

clay soil, tolerates light shade. Prone to thatch. 'Meyer', 'Flawn', 'Midwestern', 'Emerald', 'El Toro' good cultivars.

Cool-Season Grasses

Fine fescues—hard (bunch), sheep (bunch), red (sod), chewings (bunch): *Fine-textured grasses. 'Banner', 'Reliant', 'Flyer' and 'Fortress' are all excellent red fescue selections for shade, as is chewings fescue 'Jamestown'. All do best in poor soils and dislike very hot weather. Hard and sheep fescues are excellent prairie garden grasses, chewings and red fescues better lawn grasses. All take light shade. No fertilizer necessary.*

Tall fescue (Festuca elatior): *Medium-textured, deep green bunchgrass. New selections almost as pretty as Kentucky bluegrass, need only one-third to one-half the water. Best in cool climates—same regions as Kentucky bluegrass. Cultivars 'Apolo',*

Leroy takes a lazy roll in the author's buffalo grass.

gles are easier to water. There is a formula for helping you determine the watering efficiency of an area: Divide the total perimeter of the area by the square footage; if the perimeter-to-area ratio exceeds 25, the shape is inefficient.

If you are starting with bare soil, think carefully about where you really need grass in place of easy-care, water-wise alternatives. Lawn is perfect for play areas. Determine what parts of the garden would be

'Adventure', 'Falcon', 'Mustang', 'Olympic', 'Tempo', 'Houndog', 'Jaguar', 'Arid', 'Clemfine', 'Rebel', 'Apache'. Mow at 3 to 4 inches, often—this is a fast-growing grass. Tough, takes lots of traffic and light shade, especially 'Rebel'. Fertilize lightly. Tolerant of soil type and salt.

Crested wheat grass (Agropyron cristatum): *Coarse bunchgrass, very drought tolerant, salt tolerant, best for cold, dry climates. Takes light shade. Mow 3 to 4 inches. 'Fairway' and 'Ruff' denser selections; 'Ephraim' slowly forms a sod. Western wheat grass (Agropyron smithii) is an aggressive sod-forming American native with blue-green foliage.*

If you just can't bear to be without Kentucky bluegrass, a few of the more drought-tolerant selections are 'Adelphi', 'Newport', S-21, A-20, 'Enoble', 'Majestic', 'America' and 'Merion'.

Waterwise Lawn Alternatives

These lawn substitutes all spread to form a carpet. They can take some traffic, but not rough play. Plant small plants 6 inches apart. They are excellent as companions for small bulbs.

Dwarf pussytoes (Antennaria parvifolia): ❶*Has evergreen silver foliage in small rosettes. It blooms in small, fuzzy cream or pink flower clusters in spring or early summer. Do not mow; use shears or a weedwhacker to remove spent flower stems. Completely hardy.*

Horseshoe vetch (Hippocrepis comosa): *Forms a 3-inch-high mat of small pinnate leaves and 1-inch clusters of pealike yellow flowers in spring and early summer. Mow after bloom.*

Roman chamomile (Anthemis [Chamaemelum] nobilis): ❶*Has lush green, finely dissected, almost mossy leaves, evergreen in most climates. When walked upon, the foliage releases a sweet, fruity fragrance, a bit applelike. Flowers are small white daisies in spring or early summer. A nonblooming selection, 'Treneague', and a double-flowered form with white pompomlike blossoms are available. Without mowing, grows to 6 inches, can be mowed to 1 inch. Hardy to at least –20° F.*

Strawberry clover or O'Connor's legume (Trifolium fragiferum): *Has pink or white, rounded cloverlike flower heads in spring or early summer. Beware of bees. It must be planted from seed in fall. Can be mowed to 2 inches or left natural at 4 to 6 inches.*

Thyme (Thymus spp.): *Includes several low-growing, 1- to 4-inch-tall evergreen groundcovers with tiny fragrant foliage and small pink, rose, purple or white flower clusters. These attract bees, so be careful. Mow to 1 to 2 inches after flowering. The following, except the first, are all completely hardy. Thymus herba-barona, caraway thyme, has rose-pink flowers in early summer.*

Thymus pseudolanuginosus, woolly thyme, requires no mowing at all because it stays so low. The foliage is densely woolly and gray-green, and it rarely blooms. Thymus praecox spp. arcticus, mother-of-thyme, grows 3 to 6 inches with lavender or white flowers. Thymus serpyllum, lemon thyme, is similar, with more reddish flowers.

Woolly yarrow (Achillea tomentosa): *Has evergreen, finely cut gray foliage and bright yellow flowers in spring or early summer. It can be mowed after flowering to 2 to 3 inches. Completely hardy. Woolly yarrow is fire-retardant.*

---

best for entertaining, lounging, romping. You might reduce your lawn area further by putting in a patio, gazebo or deck for outdoor activities instead of grass. Add containers overflowing with lush plants and gay flowers for interest. In place of lawn where there is foot traffic, you might consider a path of stone, brick, wood, mulch or some other nonliving material. Narrow strips such as those commonly found along sidewalks and driveways are

Your Dog and Your Lawn

No matter what you've heard, a dog's urine will brown and eventually kill grass. Females are said to be worse, but what is actually happening is that the male is burning vertical plants such as shrubbery as he sprays while the female concentrates hers on the lawn in a squat. When a male dog squats rather than sprinkles, his is just as bad. Do not add baking soda to your dog's water; it can make your dog more prone to urinary tract infections and kidney stones. Green touch-up paint for lawns is a temporary solution. For a long-term solution, train your dog to go in a mulched area with no grass. It will take some effort. You will need to be consistent about escorting him or her to that special spot every time (including those dreaded midnight trips) and lavishing a great deal of praise, until the dog starts going there on his own. The training period can last anywhere from several weeks to several months, depending on your tenacity and the IQ of your dog, but it is well worth it.

difficult to mow or water efficiently. A rule of thumb is, any area less than 16 feet wide is inefficient for lawn. Plant such areas with water-wise, lower-maintenance plants. Overly shaded or fiercely hot and dry spots are also prime candidates for lawn alternatives more

suited to such conditions. Slopes are notoriously difficult to water evenly and well (see page 16). Convert these problem areas to attractive plantings of tough groundcovers, shrubs, perennials or any combination of these.

Think of the lawn as an attractive, living outdoor carpet for areas of heavy use, so it becomes a choice with a function instead of the major component of your garden's design. You will be well on the way to a more easily maintained, more environmentally friendly, waterwise garden. For the area you decide to keep as lawn, select a grass species that suits your climate and needs rather than the most common, greatest water consumer of them all, Kentucky bluegrass. Do you need tough, durable turf for heavy traffic and rough play? Do you want a refined, formal look where you'll be sitting and socializing? Do you need a shade-tolerant grass? Grasses vary in their color and texture, in the amount of water, fertilizer and mowing they need and in the climate and soil they prefer.

The two main categories of grasses are warm- and cool-season grasses. Warm-season grasses must have warm weather, preferably 80° to 95° F. to germinate and grow, and they go dormant—a tawny beige—as soon as the weather gets cold. Plant them in late spring or early summer. Cool-season grasses germinate and grow best in cool weather, 55° to 75° F. remaining green much longer than their warm-season counterparts. They tend to be more shade tolerant and more durable under traffic, and they usually require more water. Plant them in spring or early fall. Kentucky bluegrass is the most well-known cool-season grass. It is durable and beautiful, but responds to the slightest drought by going dormant. It needs close to 40 inches of water to stay green, making it a poor choice for an attractive, waterwise lawn.

Grasses differ in how they grow, some in bunches, some as spreading sod. Sod-forming grasses form denser, more uniform turf. Bunchgrasses allow more weeds to grow up between them, but are ideal for unmowed "natural" areas, mixed with perennials for a prairie effect. Bunchgrasses must be sprigged or seeded, not sodded.

SELECTING PLANTS

Now you are ready for the most enjoyable part of designing your garden: choosing the plants. No matter where you live, there is a plethora of wonderful water-wise plants from which to choose. A word about hardiness zones: Use them as a rough guide, not as the last word. These zones are assigned numbers and represent geographical areas that share similar average minimum temperatures. The catch with relying on zones is that while minimum temperatures often do predict the success or failure of a particular plant, much more is at play. Maximum temperatures, humidity, microclimates, wind desiccation, excess moisture during the dormant season and drought when a plant is first getting established play just as large a part. Hardiness zones are most helpful when selecting woody plants—trees, shrubs and vines—as these keep a woody framework above ground all year 'round that is subject to the vagaries of temperature. The warming sun of a late winter's day may break dormancy in a twig, branch or trunk. Then comes a night of freezing temperatures, and the plant is left defenseless. Winterkill often results. However, herbaceous plants that die down to the ground each year—biennials, bulbs and perennials—are protected by the soil during their dormant period, and so are much less likely to be as affected by extreme temperature fluctuations. Across the continent, a multitude of plants prove over and over again that they can thrive in gardens where they aren't supposed to, making mockery of zone designations. If in doubt, try the plant. Few herbaceous plants are that much of an investment of money or time that you can't afford to play gardener's Russian roulette now and then. And if the plant doesn't survive in one spot in your garden, try another. I follow the rule of threes—a herbaceous plant is tried in three spots before I give up on it (unless I decide that it's really quite hideous after all).

TREES

When designing your waterwise garden, the first plants to consider are trees, for they are your greatest investment in money and time. Trees have great dignity and grace, and give the garden voice by inviting birds. The cooling shade of deciduous trees is invaluable, especially on the south, southwest or west side of the garden during the hottest times of the year. In winter when the trees are without leaves, they allow desirable sunlight to filter through their branches. Evergreens offer year-'round color and serve as excellent barriers to harsh winds and undesirable views, as well as living fences for privacy. Trees casting shade over patios, walks or walls help keep these hard surfaces from getting too hot in the sun.

Generally speaking, few trees are able to withstand severe lack of water. In drought-ridden regions of the world, few trees grow except along stream and river banks, in swales and by underground springs. Keep this in mind if you live in a dry climate and are designing a garden with areas that will never receive additional water.

In those instances, you will need to plant your trees where you can get supplementary water to them; otherwise, they will not do well. Still, many trees can thrive when given only occasional thorough waterings. Choose deep-rooted trees, for these tend to be drought-tolerant. Also, deep tree roots are less likely to rob other plants of food, water and space, thus making the ground beneath such a tree more welcome for a shady planting. Don't fall for a tree simply because it grows quickly; most fast-growing trees are notoriously weak-wooded, at best leaving a sea of twigs on the ground for you to pick up after the slightest wind, and at worst, dropping a huge limb on your garden, house or car. These instant-gratification trees tend to be short-lived, often beginning to die back, decline and become insect-riddled and diseased after only a decade or two. Plant for the future.

Be sure to give the tree ample room. One of the hardest things to do is to plant a meager-looking sapling yards away from other trees or buildings—it looks so lonesome and forlorn. However, you will be doing the tree a favor if you give it the space it needs to develop its natural width and height fully. Contrary to tradition, recent studies have shown that you should not amend the soil in a tree's planting hole unless you have completely unmanageable soil such as cementlike caliche. Nor should you dig the hole deeper than the depth of the container or rootball. Make a wide hole instead, loosening the existing soil for good root penetration. The old way—a deep hole filled with fluffy, light, highly nutritious soil—causes a tree to restrict its roots to only that hole, not venturing out farther. This creates an unstable tree easily blown over by wind, and a dependent tree too, for its small root system isn't able to search for water outside its limited perimeter. Another problem with the deep hole filled with amended soil is that it promotes settling once the tree is planted, and after a few months the tree may be planted too deeply and can suffocate.

Another traditional practice,

An icy blue Colorado spruce serves as an ethereal backdrop to this garden high in the Rocky Mountains.

that of staking, has also been recently questioned. Unless the tree has a very small root system as compared to its top, or if you are planting in an extremely windy area, don't stake the tree. Studies show that unstaked trees grow stronger, stouter trunks and better root systems. Besides, stakes and guy wires are unsightly and can be unsafe if you don't look where you are walking, so there's good reason to abandon them.

The best time to plant most trees is at the end of the dormant season, just before they have begun active growth, or if the dormant season is not too cold or too hot, just before it begins, when top growth has slowed yet roots continue to grow. Smaller, younger plants are quicker to adapt to a site and suffer less shock from transplanting than larger, more mature individuals.

As you begin to select other plants—shrubs, vines, perennials—to flesh out your garden, you may feel overwhelmed by the number of choices. It is easy to be seduced by plants in brilliant bloom at the nursery or garden center. Think about what a plant will do for the garden the rest of the year. Consider long bloom time, good foliage, colorful bark or fruit and interesting form. Few plants offer all of these attributes, but they should offer more than just two weeks of flowers and then nothing of interest. Select plants that bloom at different times. Look for plants with pleasing fragrance and those that attract birds, bees or butterflies into the garden.

FINDING WATERWISE PLANTS

You may see a number of intriguing plants but be unfamiliar with their water requirements. Each year, many newcomers come available. From the wild landscapes around us, more and more beautiful plants are being tried and tamed for gardens. Beware of plants dug from the wild; insist on nursery-propagated plants. Not only are you doing the environmentally sound thing by not contributing to the endangerment and possible extinction of a wild species, you are also not risking breaking ever-stricter laws, and you are much more likely to have success with a nursery-grown plant. Wild-dug plants often have a difficult time making the transition to garden conditions. Many times they are already stressed and well on the way toward an early demise in pots at the nursery, long before you get your hands on them. A plant grown from cuttings or seed taken from the wild has adapted to containers and to various soil and water conditions at the nursery, so it is much more prepared to tolerate the big change when planted in your garden. Aside from new natives, each year numerous unusual plants from distant lands are made available to the gardener.

Whether you are trying a regional native or a new import, the best way to find out its water requirements is to learn where it grows in the wild. If it comes from a dry place, most likely it will be waterwise, unless it grows along the few bodies of water in that region. Some plants may hark from places that have plentiful water at some times of the year and severe drought at others. These plants may still be excellent candidates for the waterwise garden. Some of them go dormant during very dry periods, as is the case with many of the bulbs.

When a plant is labeled "native," it isn't necessarily well suited to a waterwise garden. Some native plants are not very drought-tolerant. Most woodland wildflowers from both the eastern and western forests of this continent require a good deal of moisture to thrive. Plants from more open areas such as meadows and fields may be more adapted to dry conditions, but a large number prefer a moisture-retentive soil high in humus. Even if a native plant comes from a dry region,

When grown in rich soil, Crocosmia 'Lucifer'—a bulbous plant favored by hummingbirds—gets by on little water.

it may grow in the moistest sites available there. Just because a plant is native doesn't necessarily mean it is a better, more adaptable garden plant than an import. We are lucky that more and more native plants are being considered and grown for garden use; not too long ago, even the most beautiful were pushed aside in favor of exotics. The rich diversity of plants now available should excite any gardener. But the pendulum always tends to swing too far. Dismissed as weeds not too long ago, natives suddenly are politically correct, the panacea for every garden—in some cases to the rigid exclusion of nonnatives. "Buy American" may be a worthy cause for clothing or automobiles, but not necessarily for our gardens.

Native plants do offer the assurance that they are adapted to your regional climate and natural rainfall. But the rumor that native plants are somehow less plagued by insects and diseases is a myth. Insects and diseases evolve along with their hosts. Consider the many plagues of the Eastern dogwood and hemlock. While certain newly introduced plants may be irresistible to pests, much like a new special at the local diner, most pests, like the diner's regular patrons, soon go back to their old favorites.

What's more, plants know no political boundaries. Why is a New Jersey native necessarily best for a New Jersey garden? What really matters is to find out where in New Jersey the plant thrives—along the sandy coastal dunes, in the Pine Bar-

rens or farther upstate in deciduous woodland, all areas with very different conditions. Native plants, like plants the world over, are adapted to a set of conditions. Some plants have a broad tolerance; these make the most tractable garden subjects, the so-called "brown thumb" plants that take talent to kill. Others have highly specific needs. Take some of our lovely western native lupines and penstemons, for example. One species may grow on one side of a hill, while another thrives on the other side due to a different soil preference. The lupine that grows wild in a sandy acidic soil will not do well in the more neutral clay of a garden just a county or two over, even though the garden may still be in the same state to which the lupine is native. Suffice it to say you should seek out plants that like the particular conditions your garden can offer them, be they native plants or imports.

If you have your heart set on a particular plant but can't seem to find it, use one or more of the several excellent references available to help you locate sources for hard-to-find plants. Small, obscure mail-order operations run by dedicated horticulturists often more for love than for money are some of the finest sources for unusual plants. Be persistent. Badger your local nursery and garden centers. They won't carry it if they don't think anyone wants to buy it. And then, you can always grow the plants on your own; plant societies and botanical gardens offer a much wider variety of seeds

This happy marriage of waterwise perennials balloon flower, daylily and prairie gayfeather is irresistible to butterflies.

On the parched plains of western Nebraska, native Thelesperma filifolium *gilds the summer landscape as far as the eye can see.*

than most commercial pursuits, and you're bound to have some luck procuring that special species from these sources.

If you can't find out much about the origins and cultural requirements of a particular plant that catches your fancy, look for some physical characteristics that give clues to low water demand. You can learn to recognize features common to many waterwise plants. Plants have developed a great

Mediterranean Mt. Etna broom, Mexican pineapple sage and silver daisy bush from New Zealand join to create a cosmopolitan waterwise composition.

Attractive foliage with diverse adaptations to drought makes up this picture: spiny thistle, waxy succulent sedum, furry silver lamb's ear and fine-textured blue sheep's fescue.

many ingenious ways to help them deal with the harsh realities of drought. The spines of cacti and spurges protect the plants against thirsty marauders eager for a nibble at their juicy stems, and trap precious dew and shade the plant to boot. Many drought-tolerant plants have developed similar prickles and thorns for the same reasons. Strongly aromatic leaves also serve as deterrents to possible predators; while we may like the fragrances of the herbs lavender, rosemary or thyme, they don't appeal to most damaging insects or herbivores. The foliage of many drought-tolerant plants is small, finely dissected, narrow or needlelike, cutting down on surface area from which moisture would be lost. Some plants have gone so far as to have little if any foliage at all, with green trunks and stems to carry out the functions of the absent leaves, such as Mormon tea (*Ephedra* spp.) and many of the brooms (*Cytisus* spp., *Genista* spp. and *Spartium* spp.).

Leaves may be covered by a pelt of hairs, as in lamb's ears; a layer of wax, as in many spurges; or a sticky resin, as in some rockrose species. These adaptations all conserve moisture by deflecting sunlight and wind, trapping or channeling water droplets and reducing evaporation from inside the leaf itself. Hairs, felt and wax often give these plants a silver, gray or blue cast; these foliage colors are easy tipoffs for identifying water-conserving plants. The rosettes of aloe, yucca and agave species funnel water down toward the roots. Succulent leaves and stems like those of iceplants and sedums store water, as do bulbs, tuberous roots and fleshy rhizomes such as those of bearded iris, peonies and daylilies. In heavy clay soil subject to drought, plants typically develop long carrotlike taproots to search deep for water, while in looser, more sandy soil, dense, widespreading fibrous root systems serve plants better by trapping water quickly as it percolates down. Think of the pretty California poppy as a prime example of a drought-adapted plant. Its orange sap is distasteful to most predators; its foliage is finely cut and blue-gray, conserving the plant's internal moisture. Beneath the ground, a long, fleshy taproot probes for water stores deep in the soil—a perfect plant for the waterwise garden.

BULBS AND ANNUALS

Once you have selected shrubs, vines and perennials for your garden, you can fill in with bulbs and annuals. These two groups of plants play the role of seasonal splash. Many bulbous plants have a long period of dormancy when neither flower nor leaf is visible above ground. This attribute helps make so many of them tolerant of dry conditions. The growing season of most bulbs consists of a few weeks of wondrous bloom followed by a period of only foliage before going completely dormant; or less often, the foliage appearing alone for some time first, then dying down, and later flowers, unaccompanied by foliage, arising for brief bloom. Bulb foliage often is not particularly attractive. As it starts to die down, it becomes downright ugly, but you should not remove it before it is completely dead, for these leaves form the sustenance in the bulb that produces the next floral display. A few bulbous plants such as arums, calla lilies and caladiums do possess good, long-lasting foliage, but these tend to have their origins in moist tropical or temperate forests, making them less than ideal for the water-wise garden. So, unlike other garden plants from which you expect beauty most of the year, bulbs are to be stuffed in and among the mainstays of the garden—through groundcovers, at the base of shrubs, between perennials—so that they can rise to the occasion and then unobtrusively sink back down once they have done their bit.

By definition, annuals live only one growing season. It can be their intrinsic nature that drives them to die after setting seed, or too cold a climate, or the gardener's desire to grow them only seasonally. In any case, they have a showy, short life in the garden. In a young garden, annuals fill gaping holes before the longer-lived plants have matured, helping the impatient gardener through the first scrawny season or two. They are indispensable for stretching the flowering season, for they tend to bloom much longer than most woody plants or perennials. They are often easy and unexacting when it comes to care, and their short life affords you the opportunity to experiment and change. Some are native to areas short on water, where they burst into a few weeks of glorious bloom after seasonal rains and then set seed for next year. Many of these are low-maintenance, for they self-perpetuate dependably. Let these lovely annual wildflowers of the

Tough little lipstick-pink Tulipa humilis *is framed by a muted backdrop of silver and gray-green leaves in early spring.*

desert loose in your garden, unencumbered by your master plan or carefully drawn design. They will pop up in the most unexpected, delightful places, bringing a sparkle of color year after year from self-sown seed.

WATERING ZONES

The plants you have chosen for your waterwise garden now need to be placed and combined to create a pleasing picture. But more importantly, they need to be grouped into areas of similar water need. Those that require the most additional irrigation are best planted closest to the water source to make watering easy and efficient. This area is sometimes appropriately called the oasis zone. Those left to fend for themselves with only natural rainfall can enhance the far reaches of your property. One or more intermediate zones fall between these two extremes. The fewer the zones, the simpler the watering. Watering zones are not a new idea, just common sense. At a well-run nursery or greenhouse, plants that need frequent watering are kept together, separate from those that may be in danger of rotting from too much water. The same rules apply in the garden. This way you keep each plant healthy by giving it what it needs—not too much, not too little—and you avoid wasting water while reducing the amount of time and effort needed to maintain your garden.

A kaleidoscope of waterwise annuals enlivens a year-old garden where perennials and shrubs are yet too small to provide much impact.

THE WATERWISE PLANTING AND GROWING GUIDE

By designing a garden with drought-tolerant plants, with water zones for plants of similar moisture requirements and a limited or modified lawn area, you have already won half the battle of conserving water. The other half involves practical, down-in-the-dirt approaches to water-wise gardening. These will help you save water and effort once you are ready to put the plans to work.

SOIL

Before you decide exactly which plants you want, get to know your soil. This way, you'll know what the plants are up against and can make any improvements necessary before planting. There are two philosophies that apply to all but the most difficult soils. One is to amend the soil with various additives to create something as close as possible to that much sought-after ideal, garden loam—rich, water-retentive, yet light and fluffy. Now you can grow a vast range of plants. The other philosophy is to leave your soil pretty much alone except perhaps to loosen it a bit with some light cultivation, and then go about finding plants that like it as it is. Your selection of plants will probably be more limited than if you had gone to great lengths to prepare perfect loam, but you have saved yourself a lot of backbreaking work. With the most difficult soils—raw subsoil, caliche, sticky clay or pure sand, you have no choice but to do some heavy work. In cases of sand or subsoil, you'll need to remove some and bring in soil and organic matter in large amounts to replace it, mixing with the top few inches of the layer remaining. Whenever you import soil, be sure to look into its source. Serious weed problems, or worse, residual herbicides brought in with soil can wreak havoc with a new planting. Caliche, a cementlike layer of soil common in the Southwest, requires serious effort as well. You can break up and excavate holes or areas to be planted and fill them with good soil, or you can build raised beds above the hardpan. Your choice of strategy will depend on the strength of available bodies and/or machinery, and the thickness of the caliche layer.

Parts of your property may have different soil types, whether naturally occurring or caused by that ultimate enemy of soil, the building process. Soils differ in nutrient content, relative acidity or alkalinity (referred to by a scale called pH), water-holding capacity and porosity—relative looseness or compaction. These parameters affect what type of plants will grow and how well. If you are starting from scratch,

Blue avena grass and seakale cool down flame-colored Siberian wallflower in the author's waterwise garden.

Clay soil

Sandy soil

Loamy soil

consider doing a soil test. Many state universities offer an inexpensive soil testing service; the kits and instructions are usually available through your county extension office. If no such service is available in your area, it is worth purchasing a small soil testing kit and doing it yourself. The results will help you determine how acid or alkaline your soil is. A range between 6 and 7.5 is considered good for most plants; much lower or higher and you might consider amending it with pH-altering soil additives. Also, most kits will give you information on the fertility levels of your soil, helping you decide if fertilizer is warranted, and if so, which and how much. Of the three major plant nutrients, nitrogen (N), phosphorus (P) and potassium (K), P and K are most important for fighting water stress. They foster good roots and sturdy, hardy growth. Iron has also been connected with increased drought hardiness. Most drought-tolerant plants are not particularly fond of extra fertilizer, especially one high in N, and many are tolerant of an alkaline pH, higher than 7.

Next, determine how well-drained your soil is. There is a big difference between good water retention and waterlogging. To see how your soil responds to water, dig a hole 18 inches by 18 inches and fill it with water. It should drain completely in 12 hours. If a little is left, you have a slow-draining soil and will need to be careful not to overwater. If the water drains very fast, within the first hour, you have

an overly fast-draining soil that will devour water at the expense of your plants. It is too loose and sandy and needs organic matter to support a wide variety of plants.

If a sizeable amount of water remains in the hole, you have a serious drainage problem and need to determine the cause—compaction, heavy clay makeup or an impermeable layer of subsoil—to choose the appropriate remedy. Even if your soil drains well, it is good to know what texture it has: clay, loamy, sandy or gravelly. Texture affects the choice of plants, and how much and often you'll need to water. No soil texture is ideal, not even the famous loam. Every plant has its preference. Loam is the most popular among plants, but you can find a large variety of plants that thrive in sand, clay or gravelly soil.

Water a small area and let it drain to the point of being moist, not muddy. Now dig up a handful and feel the texture. If it feels silky smooth, almost slippery or is slightly sticky, and can be molded easily into a thin cigar shape, you have a soil high in silt or clay, probably fairly fertile and with good, often excessive, water-holding properties. Silty or clayey soil has its own characteristics. When completely dry, such a soil, with its hard, smooth surface, is difficult to wet; water has trouble penetrating and tends to run off. Once thoroughly wet, however, the soil retains water; you need to irrigate less frequently than with other soil types.

Water tends to travel side-

ways rather than downward in clay, staying somewhat shallow, so be vigilant about watering deeply to promote good roots and to prevent salt buildup, a common problem in improperly irrigated clay soils. Clay soils are dense, heavy and easily compacted and damaged, especially when wet. You should be careful about running machinery of any kind over or through such a soil, and keep foot traffic to a minimum. Clay soils hold on to water for a long time and can become waterlogged, drowning plants by depriving their roots of air. By adding coarse, fibrous organic material such as pine needles, shredded leaves or bark, you improve the aeration of clay soils, letting water and air get in and through the soil better. Many drought-tolerant plants are highly adaptable to clay soils, however, and resent the extra humus and nitrogen that organic matter brings. Consider this when you decide which plants you want to grow. Clay soils stay cooler than other soils, a boon in hot climates and a problem in colder ones.

If the moist soil feels rough to the touch and crumbles instead of making a cigar, you have a sandy soil. Sandy soils drain well, sometimes too quickly, and tend to be nutrient-poor. Water percolates too fast, straight downward, leaching nutrients out with it before plants have a chance to absorb them. Such soils need to be watered more often than a clay soil, but require less water each time. Sandy soils also benefit from the addition of organic matter, which in this case

---

WATER AND SOIL TYPE COMPARISON

Water-holding capacity in 100 square feet of 1-inch-deep soil:
sandy soil: 60 gallons
loamy soil: 90 gallons
clay soil: 160 gallons

Soil depth 1 inch of water travels:
sandy soil: 12 inches
loamy soil: 7 inches
clay soil: 4 inches

Average water intake in inches per hour before runoff:
sandy soil: .8 inch bare; 1.3 inch with sod; 1.5 inch with organic mulch
loamy soil: .4 inch bare; .8 inch with sod; 1.0 inch with organic mulch
clay soil: .25 inch bare; .5 inch with sod; .8 inch with organic mulch

---

binds the soil together like a sponge, holding water and food. Use well-decomposed, finer-textured sources of organic matter for sand, such as aged leaf mold, manure or compost. Sandy soil is more amenable to tilling and trampling, and tends to warm up quickly.

If your soil is full of small stones, you have a gravelly soil, which is generally well-drained and very poor in terms of nutrition. Again, organic matter can help alleviate these problems. Organic matter really does work in these seemingly contradictory ways. A rule of thumb is to add about one-third the depth of the amended soil; for example, add a 6-inch layer of organic matter to an 18-inch-deep area. It is not the perfect solution, however, for it depletes readily and should be replenished every year or two, and a good many drought-adapted plants dislike it.

If you grab a bit of moist soil and can make a fat cigar but not a cigarillo with it, you have reached the closest thing to soil nirvana—you have loam.

Adding organic matter, loosening or cultivating the soil by turning or tilling, or aerating it with a fork or core-aerating machine all improve soil percolation. With most waterwise plants, this is more important than any other aspect of soil preparation; These plants do best when they have access to the water they need without waterlogging. When a soil can absorb between ½ to 1 inch of water an hour, it ideally balances water retention and percolation.

Recently, water-holding polymers have come onto the market. These small crystals or beads absorb and store up to 400 times their weight in water, making the moisture available to plants as they need it rather than allowing it to run off or waterlog the soil. One pound of these unusual substances will hold between 15 pounds and 40 pounds of water. Ideally, these make the perfect water-saving soil additive. However, plants vary a great deal in their ability to get water from the crystals: Some mine it well, others have trouble getting any. Also, temperature and salt content of the soil affect the water-holding capacity of the polymers, and some become ineffective after a short time. The most promising—cross-linked polyacrylamides—are proving to have long-lasting effectiveness, up to 10 years and beyond. They have been shown to absorb soluble nutrients, reducing loss through leaching. Sandy soils are especially improved by the crystals' ability to hold and make available to plants water that would otherwise percolate down and away. Clay soils appear to benefit from the physical expanding and contracting of the crystals, which loosens the soil and improves water and air infiltration. In tests, irrigation frequency of treated turf is reduced by 20 percent to 40 percent. The most efficient way to incorporate the crystals into a planting is at the outset during soil preparation, but they can be applied later with the help of a compressed-air injection gun. At this early point in the development and study of these seemingly magic crystals, they are best suited to help establish a new planting and for containers. If you plan to incorporate them into the soil, be careful to keep them away from paths, patios or foundations, for they expand and contract a great deal. These synthetic polymers are said to be inert, but the jury is still out on what long-term effects their residues may have in the soil once they break down.

Organic Matter, Mulches and Soil Additives: Pros and Cons

ORGANIC MATTER/ ORGANIC MULCHES

All break down and serve as soil additives and conditioners. *For mulch, the fresher the source, the more likely it will burn the plants. The best additives and mulches encourage symbiotic microbes, helping plants grow better. However, organic materials are also favorite hideaways for pests such as earwigs, sowbugs, slugs and cutworms. Remember, do not add organic matter to planting holes for trees, or to soil to be planted with natives that dislike a rich soil high in nitrogen.*

Shredded leaves— *excellent mulch and soil conditioner. Readily available, inexpensive or free. Natural-looking. May acidify or make soil more alkaline, depending on source of leaves. May mat or compact; avoid thin-leaved sources such as maple, and use tougher, less pliable foliage such as oak. May blow away. May harbor rodents.*

Grass clippings— *compost first before adding to soil. Dry first before using as a mulch. Readily available, inexpensive or free. Decompose quickly. May mat down, may burn plants as they decompose. Need to add nitrogen. May contain weed seeds or harmful herbicide residue. Better to leave them on lawn anyway.*

Straw— *readily available, inexpensive. Best as a mulch, not a soil conditioner. Easy to apply. Weed seeds may be a problem, rodents too. May blow away. Fire hazard.*

Pine needles— *best as a mulch. Sometimes readily available. Attractive, quite long-lived. May blow away. May acidify soil. Fire hazard.*

Composted leaves, leaf mold— *best soil additive. Not a good mulch—break down too quickly.*

Garden compost— *a great soil additive but not a mulch—breaks down too quickly. Weed seeds may be a problem.*

Peat— *not good as a mulch—makes an impenetrable crust when dry. Expensive. Blows or washes away, breaks down quickly. Environmentally unsound because it is a nonrenewable resource; peat mining threatens ecosystems. Excellent as an additive in container soils. Occasionally high in salt.*

Ground bark, bark chips— *best as a mulch—attractive, natural-looking, easy to apply. Can be expensive. Be sure to get a good size; bark too finely ground will mat and become impenetrable to air and water, or blow away; too large, and it won't cover the ground without gaps and is rough and messy-looking. May need to add nitrogen fertilizer in warm, humid areas where bark breaks down more quickly. As a soil additive, must add nitrogen.*

Wood chips, chipper waste— *best as a mulch, but will need to add nitrogen. If too finely ground, will break down rapidly, or blow or wash away.*

Manure— *excellent soil additive, not a good mulch—breaks down too rapidly. Can be cheap and readily available in nonurban areas. Be sure it is aged at least one year and no longer smells strong or warms up when in a pile, otherwise may burn plants. Weed seed can be a problem. Avoid feedlot manure—high in salt, will burn. Barnyard manure is best.*

Nut and grain hulls, coarsely ground corn cobs, other agricultural by-products— *sometimes nice mulch materials. Add nitrogen. May blow away, may be contaminated with chemicals. Not usually the best choice for a soil additive.*

Sawdust— *not recommended as a mulch—fire hazard, may mat down or blow or wash away. Can be used as a soil additive but must add nitrogen. Readily available, cheap.*

INORGANIC MULCHES

These don't break down nearly as rapidly, if at all, and thus are good only as mulches, not as soil additives, with the exception of vermiculite and perlite. Most are more expensive than the majority of organic mulches. These mulches are energy-intensive—rock sources must be mined and hauled; plastics are petroleum products.

Rocks, pebbles, gravel— *many colors available. Often expensive. Difficult to spread and move when adding more plants, so best for permanent, unchanging landscapes. Weeds grow through easily—best to combine with a landscape fabric beneath. May roll down a slope. May reflect heat onto plants and nearby spaces, which can be used to advantage under deciduous trees and shrubs—the plants' foliage shades the mulch during the hot season, keeping it cool, yet in winter, when the plants are leafless, the sun reaches the mulch and heats it.*

Gravel is an excellent mulch for plants, such as this euphorbia, which resent the humus created by organic mulches.

Lava rock—*lightweight, easier to apply than rocks. Can be expensive. Same problems as rocks. Decomposes faster.*

Decomposed granite, brick chips, marble chips, clay aggregate—*regionally available, can be expensive. Variety of colors. Neat, formal appearance. Same problems as with rock mulches.*

Sand—*do not use as a mulch or garden soil additive. It will turn heavy soil to concrete unless added in huge quantities. Works well as a soil additive in containers.*

Black or clear plastic—*avoid unless in an unplanted area, where it can be used to suppress weeds (cover with a more attractive mulch on top). No water or air passes through and intense heat is created underneath; this kills off beneficial soil life and may promote the growth of soil-borne diseases.*

Landscape fabric/woven polypropylene—*lets air and water pass but not weeds. Good on slopes to retard runoff and erosion. Expensive. Need to cover with another mulch for attractive appearance.*

Vermiculite and perlite—*expensive, lightweight. Do not use as a mulch—will blow or wash away. Good soil aerators, excellent for container soil mixes. Perlite is white and can look unnatural when mixed in the garden soil, but is longer-lasting than tawny-gray vermiculite. Vermiculite absorbs water better than perlite.*

Making Compost

Compost is the essence of recycling, in which plant refuse is turned back into a soil-like material, humus. Finished compost is odorless, dark, soft and crumbly, perfect for your garden.

Compost is a complex, living ecosystem; bacteria, fungi, insects, worms and other creatures work their magic, turning twiggy prunings, kitchen scraps and peelings, coffee and tea grounds, fallen leaves, spent flower stems and uprooted weeds into black gold.

Don't ship off such potentially useful materials to the ever-expanding and overfilled dump. Compost helps aerate your soil, makes it more water-retentive, enhances root development and serves as a storehouse of nutrients and other substances beneficial to plant growth— enzymes, vitamins, acids, growth hormones and the like. With an annual top-dressing of compost, your garden needs less, if any, fertilizer. Compost takes the place of peat—an expensive, less renewable resource—as a superior soil additive. To boot, compost has been shown to improve plant color, resistance to insects and disease, and the shelf life and nutritional content of vegetables and fruits.

Compost comes free, but not without a little work. New studies suggest mixing rather than layering the ingredients. A pile 4 feet tall and wide is large enough to support the breakdown process yet small enough to be man-ageable. If you are in a hurry, turn the pile with a fork or shovel on a weekly basis to aerate it, and keep it moist but not soggy. If you can wait several months to a year for the finished product, then you don't need to do anything to the pile. In time, it too will become "black gold" without any intervention on your part. Adding soil or manure speeds the process, as does incorporating a bit of finished compost into a fresh pile. An equal ratio of soft green and dry woody materials makes for faster, better compost.

Grinding coarse ingredients with a chipper or lawn mower speeds composting, as does enclosing the pile in a slatted bin, tumbler or wire mesh cylinder. Such enclosures keep out scavengers, look neater and hold the pile in place against strong winds.

Weed seeds are often a problem, for it takes well-distributed high temperatures to kill them and most piles are not that efficient. If you don't put weeds that have gone to seed in the pile, you avoid the problem. Be sure not to add any meat, bones, dairy products or fat to your compost. Also, don't add diseased plant debris to the pile.

WATERING

To save the most water, the best thing you can do beyond good design is to irrigate appropriately and efficiently. This means watering in ways that minimize waste from runoff, overapplication and evaporation. It also means watering deeply and thoroughly to encourage a large, deep root system that can mine the soil more successfully for available water, is less susceptible to temperature extremes and supports the plant more strongly against soil erosion and wind.

Regardless of how you plan to irrigate, be sure to water only when your plants need it, not by any artificial calendar or clock. You may have heard of the so-called ET or evapotranspiration rate, a number calculated regionally representing the amount of water lost from the soil and a typical lawn or specific agricultural crop through evaporation and transpiration. Weather affects this number. Some extension services can give you conversion formulas for various types of plants to make the ET number more useful in helping you gauge the watering needs of nonturf areas in the garden.

Rather than rely on a number, become acquainted with the individual characteristics of your garden's water needs. Then you can begin to follow a rough time guideline. For instance, if you know that a particular bed dries out completely about every week during the heat of summer, water that area by the week during this time; but until you

know this about the bed, don't assume anything.

Judging when to water isn't easy. Watering well is a combination of art and science. It would be nice if each plant came with a user's manual that told you exactly how often and how much to water. Each plant is different, and water requirements vary by species. But the size of a plant is a consideration, too; a small plant with a small root system needs more frequent watering but less in amount than a larger plant of the same species, with a more developed root system. Well-established plants get by on less frequent watering than newly planted ones. An actively growing plant needs more water than a dormant plant, but not all dormant plants can survive without water. Evergreen plants especially are prone to winter desiccation by losing water through their foliage. This causes so-called winterkill more often than do low temperatures.

Another important factor affecting a plant's water requirements is the type of soil it is growing in. A porous, sandy soil needs to be watered more often than a heavy, dense, clay soil. Clay soils compact easily, their surface becoming an impervious hardpan that repels water, so you need to be extra careful with sprinklers and flooding, both of which can damage soil surface and structure. If you have a heavy soil, consider drip systems or soaker hoses instead of sprinklers. A plant's water needs are also affected by temperature, humid-

ity, time of year, sun, shade and wind. There are a few general guidelines to follow—wind, sun and heat dry out plants and soil more quickly than cool temperatures, high humidity and shade. Thus, learning how best to water your garden means getting to know your climate, your garden's microclimates, its soil and the plants.

Use your fingers to probe the soil around a plant before watering—three or four inches deep rather than just at the surface is necessary to really determine how dry the soil is. Or push a long screwdriver into the soil until it meets with resistance. That is the level of moisture penetration. Soil augers that remove a long, thin tube of soil that you can then look at and feel, and rather expensive devices called tensiometers that when stuck in the ground will determine the moisture content, are available if you feel really unsure of your touch. And, employ that old-fashioned object so faithfully and eagerly inspected by generations of farmers and gardeners alike, the trusty rain gauge. Placed out in the open, away from potential obstructions, this simplest of instruments tells you exactly how much rain or overhead irrigation your plants have received. Combine this with knowledge of your soil type, and you can make an educated guess about how deep down the soil has been moistened. Intense, heavy rains and misty sprinkles give falsely high readings in rain gauges, however—the former mainly runs off rather than soaking into the soil, while the latter evaporates before having a chance to penetrate deeply.

Let a plant's appearance tell you when it needs water. This is not to say you should wait until a plant lies limply on the ground before watering it, but there are telltale signs that signal it is time to water. It is better to wait for a plant to let you know it is in need than to overwater, but you have to be observant. When a plant's leaves begin to droop slightly or curl, these are the first signs that it needs water. The plant is trying to reduce its surface area, thus cutting down on evaporation from its foliage. However, be aware that some species, especially those with large, soft leaves, show these signs every day during the hottest times of the year or when there is a lot of sun and wind, and may actually not need water. On the other hand, if a normally pert plant is wilted first thing in the morning, you should interpret that as a real sign of drought stress. Feel the soil before watering. Once a plant shows a dullness or graying and darkening of its leaves, a sudden aging and shattering of most of its flowers, and its new growth and flower stems are sagging, it is starting to experience water stress in earnest. You have let it go a bit too far—water now and the plant will still be fine, but you may have checked its growth somewhat and reduced flowering. Once it is dropping flower buds and the lower, older foliage is yellowing, browning, drying up and falling off, the

plant is in severe drought stress. You probably will be able to save it but you should not let it get to this point. A plant this stressed is highly vulnerable to attack from insects and disease.

Some signs of overwatering, on the other hand, are yellowing, loss of the younger leaves and a wilted look similar to underwatered plants. Too much water encourages disease, especially soil-borne fungal and bacterial diseases that are notoriously difficult to treat. Root fungus attacks overwatered trees and shrubs and is generally fatal. Heavy soils high in clay are more susceptible to waterlogging, literally suffocating a plant's roots and killing it by filling the limited air spaces with water. Loose sandy soils are more forgiving, allowing water to move through more quickly.

Beyond the importance of getting to know when to water, you need to consider the best techniques available to you. If you are creating a dry land garden that depends solely on natural rainfall for irrigation, you will still need to water the young plants while they are getting established. In this case, you can probably get by with inefficient techniques like hauling watering cans and dragging hoses for the few months you'll need to be vigilant and help out.

Most waterwise gardens include at least an area or two that requires some supplemental water on a seasonal basis beyond the initial establishment period, or at the very least do best by having water

available for occasional use. No hard and fast rules apply for all regions, but generally spring is peak time for watering if rainfall or snowmelt is inadequate, for at this time plants grow strongly and need a good start before the hottest time of the year sets in. Summer is usually the hottest time, and sometimes also the driest. If you have chosen drought-tolerant plants, summer shouldn't be the most intense watering season. Many plants naturally toughen and slow their growth during this time, and some actually go partially or completely dormant, waiting for the cooler weather of autumn to resume growth. For such plants, it is critical that they receive enough water in the autumn. Winter, as mentioned before, is not a time to forget about watering entirely. In areas of dry winters with little snow cover, occasional watering is essential. So, for most waterwise gardens, having water accessible for prudent use is vital. Before deciding on a system, consider all the options available and choose one or a combination of several that best meet your and your garden's needs.

The most primitive, time-consuming way to water is manually, with a watering can or hose in hand. With a hose, it is hard to know how much water has been applied; with can or hose, water tends to come too quickly, resulting in runoff and waste. This is not to say that you should get rid of the watering can and toss the hose nozzle. For container care, the watering can is still an ex-

The small, narrow foliage of thread-leaf gaillardia, blue flax, sunrose and Salvia jurisicii *reduces surface evaporation, helping the plants stave off drought.*

cellent choice. You can deliver the water quickly and directly to the pot, and usually you won't have too far to carry the can, since most containers tend to be near the house and thus near a water tap. Cisterns that collect rainwater, usually off the roof of the house via gutters, are a good source of water to fill your can. One thousand square feet of roof harvest a remarkable 150 gallons of water from ¼ inch of rain. To control mosquitoes that would like to breed in the cistern's water, either use the water up within a day or two, cover it or float small rings that are commercially available, impregnated with an environmentally safe biological control, *Bacillus israelensis,* that kills the larvae. When you plant your containers, leave enough room between the top of the soil and the rim of the container for easy watering; otherwise you'll spill and waste a good deal, and need to pour several times to wet the soil thoroughly. For containers less than 8 inches in diameter, an inch of lip is enough. Up to about 15 inches, 2 inches will do. Larger containers 1½ feet or greater in diameter require at least a 3-inch space for efficient watering.

If you have a large number of containers placed close together, you might consider rigging a small drip irrigation system. Now all you'll need to do is turn the water on and off. You can even have liquid or soluble fertilizer added along with the water by attaching a special distributor. A drip irrigation system makes use of plastic or rubber tubing attached to the water source and fitted with smaller tubes along its length where needed to bring water to each individual plant. You can camouflage such a system by careful staging of the containers.

Manual watering has one other useful application: for watering trees. Often trees are surrounded by areas that either require less or more shallow watering than the tree or no water at all, such as mulch or a patio. To deliver the water necessary for the tree directly without waste, and deeply enough to encourage a good root system, consider using a deep-root irrigator—a long, hollow metal tube with holes along its length. This is a labor-intensive but highly effective method. Plunge the needlelike pipe into the ground about 18 inches deep and attach a hose, running water into the tube for about 30 to 60 seconds. The water goes into the pipe and seeps out the holes deep into the ground, avoiding runoff and surface evaporation, and delivering water to all levels of the tree's root system. Repeat this several times in different places beneath the crown of the tree, beginning about 1 foot outside the drip line (where the edge of the crown hangs over the ground below) to halfway back toward the trunk, since most of the tree's feeder roots are concentrated in this region. Spread applications about 1 foot apart: You'll need more closely spaced holes if your soil is sandy—the water travels more vertically than horizontally—and less if it is clay, where water spreads farther sideways. Deep-root irrigators are ideal for heavy clay soil and for trees on slopes. You can also fertilize effectively this way. If the soil is so hard that poking a tube into it at all is a huge battle, another option for efficient tree watering is to create a furrow in a ring at the edge of the tree's drip line or a shallow, basinlike depression, to fill with water from a hose. The water will slowly percolate from the moat into the soil without damaging it or running off.

No watering system is perfect. Each has its strong points and drawbacks. Climate, soil type, the hardness of your water, the shape of the garden and the plants' characteristics all determine what will work best. Water can be applied in a fine spray or mist or as a steady stream. A steady stream delivers water quickly, but unless it is caught and collected, much of the water will run off, often carrying precious soil with it. A fine spray is similar to a gentle rain—it washes the plants, removing dust and pollution; it cools the foliage and raises humidity. The soil is less likely to suffer compaction or erosion than from a stronger spray or stream, and less water is lost to runoff. A mist of water on the foliage of susceptible plants also helps control spider mites and keeps powdery mildew at bay, yet may invite other diseases such as downy mildew, black spot and botrytis. If you live in a humid climate and are growing plants prone to these diseases, you may want to avoid watering this way. In a

Tough and rampant, water-thrifty wisteria frames this formal facade with grace.

more arid, sunny climate, water spray is welcomed by the plants, but you may lose a great deal of water to evaporation unless you irrigate early in the morning or late in the evening.

Wind also affects fine spray a great deal, making it difficult to regulate where the spray hits. Often overspray occurs on hard surfaces where water then quickly runs off or simply evaporates. Fine spray is also poorly suited for watering irregularly shaped areas and densely planted beds with large perennials and shrubs, where the plant canopy catches most of the water, preventing it from hitting the soil and getting to the roots. If you increase the coarseness of the spray, you can partly overcome this problem and also remove some unwanted insects, but you may bend and break some of the plants. Also, sprinkler spray has been linked to fungal disease in the root systems of xeric plants. For all these reasons, overhead spray of any kind is best suited to areas that are larger, regular in shape and planted in turf or low-growing groundcovers of average or greater water need.

If you plan on making such an area relatively permanent, consider installing an automated stationary sprinkler system. Such a system is best installed before the garden is planted, and thus requires more initial work and expense. It is also more difficult to fix should it malfunction, or to change if you redesign part of the garden. The majority of these systems are buried. If you don't bury yours below the frost line, be sure to drain it as the frost season nears or you will have costly damage in terms of both time and money. In mild climates, such systems still tend to be beneath the ground or at least under a layer of mulch. This makes for an unobtrusive way to water but creates extra work when changes or repairs are warranted. Automated systems are ideal if you plan to go away frequently. They are a great way to water, but only if they are well suited to your garden and properly adjusted and maintained.

With an underground automated system, pop-up nozzles are perfect for a lawn or other low-growing area, for they are inconspicuous and don't get in the way of mowing or foot traffic. Keep them free of overgrown plants that might block their trajectory. Never combine galvanized pipe with bronze or brass fittings—they corrode one another and cause irreparable leaks. Rotary nozzles work well if you have good water pressure and need to irrigate a large area; large streams rotate over a wide radius, delivering between ⅛ to ½ inch of water per hour. Spray heads spread a finer sheet of water at a faster rate, over a smaller area, and need less pressure to operate. Some spray nozzles apply water at too fast a rate for the soil to absorb; choose a nozzle that makes a rather coarse, low-level spray at low pressure, a so-called low-volume spray head. Heavily thatched turf also has trouble absorbing water; consider dethatching and aerating such a lawn.

No matter what nozzle or sprinkler device you choose, you can aid absorption by cycling your water applications: Apply water until runoff begins, shut it off, and begin again later. The off-cycles should be at least twice the duration of the on-cycles. Continue these cycles until you have applied the amount needed for a deep, thorough watering of the area. Water applications in these small time increments are effective for heavy, hard-to-wet soils and for slopes, too. They are a bother to run unless you use an automated system with a timer. If you decide to go with a timer, you have freed yourself considerably. You can program when and how long the system is to irrigate. You can water during the wee hours of the morning while you sleep, the best time because evaporation rates and wind are low and yet the sun will come up soon enough to dry off the foliage, lessening the chance of fungal disease. Timers also allow you to go away without having to beg a neighbor or friend to come water. With any automation, don't become so complacent that you don't adjust the system as the seasons and the garden's water needs change. If you don't install a rain switch, be sure to turn off the system when it is raining; nothing is as ludicrously wasteful as an automated sprinkler system carrying on full force during a downpour. Electronically hooking a tensiometer into the system is the ultimate in high tech. This device senses when moisture levels reach a certain point, but you remain the initial calibrator and decision maker, no matter how complex and sensitive the system.

If you already have an automated sprinkler system in place, you can upgrade its efficiency by changing to low-volume, low-pressure spray heads with a pattern that stays low to the ground. With any system, check for clogs and leaks on a regular basis and periodically measure how much water the system delivers in a given time period so you can water for the right amount of time necessary. All overhead sprinklers should overlap their spray somewhat to compensate for lack of uniform irrigation patterns. Lastly, don't ever water with an overhead system when the sun is out in full force or when it is windy or hot.

The easiest way to determine how much and how evenly water is being delivered by a spray system is by placing several shallow containers of the same size—catfood or tuna

In difficult, dry shade, the powder blue stars of creeping bellflower and glowing foliage of golden feverfew make a lovely pair.

cans work well—in different spots under the spray pattern. Run the water for half an hour, then measure the amount of water in each can. If there is more than a ¼-inch difference, the spray is too uneven for efficiency and needs to be adjusted or altered. To figure how much water is delivered, add the water in all the containers together and divide by the number of cans, then multiply this number by 2 to get the average amount of water per hour your system delivers.

If you live in a region where rain tends to come in violent cloudbursts, you may want to harvest this water, for if left to pound your garden in quick torrents, most of it runs off. You can contour your garden by mounding the soil into berms to divert water to low-lying depressions in the soil around trees and shrubs, or to ditches and dry wells lined with drainage tile or river rock. You can make this yet more efficient by putting perforated pipe vertically into the ground at the bottom of these depressions for better water penetration. Slant the surface of walks, patios and driveways to direct water to plants or to ditches, or use porous paving material such as gravel. Cisterns, tanks and barrels can be used to store excess runoff from the roof or pavement; pumps or buried, perforated pipe attached to these storage containers help distribute the water later.

Gray water, the used water from washing machines, sinks, baths and showers, can be collected and used to irrigate. You must use no-phosphate, biode-

gradable soaps and follow other precautions if you want this to work. Local plumbing and public health codes make this a less viable option in many regions, often forcing you to add a filtering and chlorinating device, and to deliver the water underground, not allowing it to reach the surface. It is worthwhile to look into as a possibility, nevertheless.

For nonturf areas, your best choice is drip or trickle irrigation, the most water-conserving system available, saving up to 70 percent more water than conventional methods. Drip irrigation is an efficient, inexpensive and inconspicuous way to water. It applies water slowly, without the runoff, overspray and evaporation problems that plague other systems. Drip irrigation is highly versatile; you can design a system of any size or complexity to meet your needs, and you can add to or change the system whenever you want. Water is delivered directly to where you want it, which is the intelligent and thrifty way to do it. This keeps at bay weeds that would otherwise germinate in moistened bare spots receiving overspray from an overhead sprinkler. A drip system is ideally suited for watering individual plants, widely spaced plants, small or unusually shaped areas, slopes, and heavy soils with infiltration problems. By changing the number and type of emitters at the end of water tubes, you can tailor the flow rate and size of the area to be watered to meet the needs of the plants and your soil. Space emitters closer

together in sandy soils, wider apart in clay. Using miniature sprinklers and sprayers instead of the slower drip emitters allows you to use the system in larger, more thickly planted beds.

Soaker and perforated hoses ooze and spray water. They are also considered a form of drip irrigation, with similar advantages. They are somewhat more easily damaged and wear out more quickly than other drip systems, but their portability and flexibility makes them popular. Drip irrigation is also ideal for situations where strong water pressure is not dependable or lacking, for it operates at low pressure. In fact, the installation of a pressure regulator, a backflow prevention device and filter to prevent clogging are also recommended. With such a low-pressure system, a larger area can be irrigated from the same water source at the same time, and when leaks occur, as they inevitably do with any irrigation system, they don't cause as great a problem. Check for them regularly, however, to ensure that the system is working properly—one emitter that isn't doing its job means one area is not getting adequate water, which may translate into the loss of a cherished plant.

When you design a drip system for your garden, divide the garden into circuits. Each area should have the appropriate number and type of emitters for its watering needs—say, drip emitters at the drip line of a tree and in the shrub border, mini-spray emitters threaded throughout the groundcovers, mini-sprinklers in a large perennial border and a soaker or perforated hose weaving along the length of a hedge. Keep emitters away from tree trunks or the crowns of plants to avoid possible problems with rot. With large shrubs and trees, be sure to place enough emitters and spread in such a way to promote a root system large enough to anchor these plants. Be aware that slopes may affect water pressure, and design the system with obstacles, such as driveways, walls or paths that the tubing may need to circumvent, in mind.

There are few negative aspects to drip irrigation, but if you have hard water prone to mineral deposits, the system will tend to clog, even with a filter. Also, if your climate regularly surprises you with unseasonable, unexpected frosts, a drip system may be too vulnerable. If you bury the system, it will be hard to monitor for leaks. Lastly, if your soil is already on the saline side, you will need to flood it every now and then to leach out the accumulated salts, because drip irrigation waters too slowly to flush the soil adequately.

Water can be applied through the stationary systems described or via a portable system. A portable system is the least expensive option and can be changed as your garden changes, yet requires more work on your part because you will need to set it up and move it from place to place. This can mean a lot of hose-dragging and careful threading between vulnerable plants. Typical portable systems combine hoses with a variety of sprinkler attachments: pulsating or whirling heads, oscillating arms or stationary fans. The best of these deliver an even, coarse spray. None are completely uniform. A small area with sandy soil can be well-served with the fast, fanlike output of an owl-eye attachment; a clay soil needs the slower, finer spray of an oscillating spinkler, but such an attachment is more prone to evaporation and wind deflection. Pulsating attachments and the traveling-tractor type work well on flat lawns but not in tall plantings. Each attachment comes with advantages and drawbacks. Generally, portable systems are more obtrusive and unattractive than automatic systems, so you will also spend time dismantling and storing your sprinkler.

PLANTING

Few garden activities are as satisfying as planting. Before you get swept away, be sure any buried irrigation system and the hard landscape— paths, patios, rocks and the like—are in place. It is much easier to plant around these than to install them while tiptoeing around plants, or worse yet, having to dig out plants to accommodate them. A classic pitfall of the overeager planter is spacing plants too closely to each other and to structures in the impatient desire to create a mature, full effect. No matter how difficult it is to look at all that empty space in the beginning, restrain yourself and leave each plant enough room to reach its mature width and height without crowding. Overcrowded plants compete detrimentally with one another for food, light, air and water. Pests and diseases find havens among them.

Don't be tempted by the largest specimen of a plant; often a smaller plant is a much wiser investment, for it is less expensive and yet tends to establish more quickly and catch up to the larger plant by growing better. One of the nice things about creating a waterwise garden is that most of the plants will be less susceptible to planting stress, for they already have an inborn ability to handle drought. This same ability stretches the possible seasons for planting; while more water-needy plants do best when planted during the cooler, moister months of the year, a drought-tolerant plant can handle less than optimum planting conditions. Remember, though, that all plants, no matter how xeric, need some water to get started. Incorporating a slurry of cross-linked polyacrylamide crystals in the planting holes and spreading a mulch will go a long way toward keeping establishment watering to a minimum.

MULCHES

Mulches are an invaluable ally in the waterwise garden. They can beautify an area, keeping it neat and tying it together visually. Much more, a mulch makes life easier for the gardener by cutting down on watering and weeding, and it improves life for the plants. A mulch is any material, organic or inorganic, that is spread over the surface of the soil. You can add a mulch to the soil before planting or between the plants later, or you may use a mulch as a decorative alternative to plants in difficult areas. When used with plants, most mulches should be layered between 2 and 4 inches thick to maximize their effect without creating problems for the roots of the plants.

First and foremost, mulching conserves water. It reduces surface evaporation and slows runoff and its companion, erosion. In nature, plant debris often forms a natural mulch. A 2-inch layer of leaf litter on the forest floor decreases evaporation of water from the soil between 45 percent and 65 percent over bare soil. Mulches also protect soil from compaction, be it by feet, heavy rain or pounding irrigation. This in turn allows for better water penetration and air movement throughout the soil by minimizing slaking or crusting of the soil surface.

Mulching modifies temperature fluctuations, keeping a sunbaked area's soil benevolently cool, up to 10° F. lower. This helps delay premature soil warming in the spring, which can force early growth vulnerable to frost damage. When night temperatures fall way below the day's, a mulch protects the soil from experiencing these extremes, and this reduces plant stress and encourages steady, healthy growth.

If you mulch before planting an area, you protect it from the trampling that may occur during the planting process, and you keep weeds to a minimum. Applying a mulch to unplanted soil is much easier than spreading it between plants. On the downside, you'll need to work through the mulch while digging and planting. When a planting is young, mulch is priceless; it conserves water for the fledgling plants, helping them get established, and also protects their unacclimated roots from temperature extremes and possible frost heaving. By suppressing weeds, it keeps these interlopers from robbing precious water from desirable plants. Once the plants fill out, they begin to serve as their own mulches. In fact, plants themselves can be considered mulches; a groundcover or dense planting of any kind serves the soil and itself in much the same way as a layer of gravel or bark chips. If mulch is applied in areas with no plants at all, its weed-suppressing properties play an important aesthetic role.

Mulches are also a good way to create distinct zones that direct traffic away from a planting. In this way, a small mulched area around trees and shrubs protects the roots from compaction by foot and the stems and trunks from mower damage that so often causes infection, weakening and a slow demise later on. When using an organic mulch near plants with bark, keep the mulch a few inches from the trunks to prevent nesting rodents from chewing the bark and girdling the plant.

Mulches come in a wide variety, differing in availability and appearance from region to region. Each has its pros and cons (see pages 36–37). Organic mulches tend to be less expensive and easier to spread, and can improve soil fertility and structure as they break down, feeding a large population of beneficial bacteria, worms and insects. Some can help acidify an alkaline soil. Their decomposition, however, may temporarily take nitrogen from the soil, which may cause stunted growth in the plants, the symptoms of which are yellowing older or lower foliage. Overwatering and a warm, moist climate speed the decomposition process, increasing the possibility of a nitrogen deficiency. This problem is most acute with very woody, fine-textured materials such as sawdust and finely ground bark,

which are better soil additives than mulches. Add a nitrogen fertilizer to the soil as you apply them. Ammonium sulfate at a rate of 1 pound per 1-inch layer of mulch over 100 square feet is effective.

Some organic mulches, notably fresh wood chips, can burn plants as they decompose. To avoid this, make sure the mulch is aged. It should be odorless and, when in a pile, the center should not be warmer than the rest. If the mulch steams or smells, leave it in a pile and turn frequently; within a few months, the mulch should be ready to use.

As organic mulch breaks down and decomposes, you need to replenish it. Organic mulches also can be contaminated with weed seed, pests, diseases and chemical residues. You have to be more careful about the source of such mulches than with inorganic mulches. Xeric plants tend to prefer inorganic mulches, such as stone and gravel, to organic ones. Such mulches need less replenishing, but are often more expensive. They are also difficult to work around once in place for they cannot be dug into the soil. For this reason they are

better suited to plantings where little modification is expected.

Avoid using black plastic as a mulch in a planting because it keeps air and moisture from passing in and out of the soil underneath, stressing plant roots and killing beneficial organisms. Also beware of extremely light or dark colors; very light mulches like white gravel increase glare, while very dark ones intensify heat. Small, lightweight, finely ground mulches are easily blown or washed away; if not, they tend to compact into an impenetrable layer, keeping out air and water. Also, if you live in an area where fire is a hazard, choose a fire-retardant mulch.

This hot-colored summer medley of western natives—California poppies, gaillardia and blazing star—prefers no supplemental water.

LAWN PLANTING AND MAINTENANCE

For the majority of us who plan on keeping a part of the garden in turf, there are several ways to make a lawn healthier and more waterwise. Should you be faced with a serious water shortage or enforced rationing, keep in mind that when practicing irrigation triage in the garden, the lawn should go first. Most grasses can survive serious drought by going dormant, and if they do succumb, they are easier and quicker to replace than trees, shrubs and perennials. In Denver, 80 percent of household water goes to lawn watering in the summer months.

If you plan to replace the old turf with a new species of grass, you can strip the old sod with a rented sod-stripping machine or till or spade it under;

all of these options are hard work. Or, you can smother it or kill it off with glyphosate and then till under the dead sod. Once that is done, you should prepare the soil adequately. Native dryland grasses need only a bit of soil loosening and cultivating before planting, but most other grasses do best when ample amounts of organic matter are worked in to a depth of at least 8 inches, preferably deeper. Adjust the pH if necessary. Grade the area as flat as possible—berms and slopes are difficult to water and mow. Grade the soil level a little lower than adjacent hard surfaces to catch water runoff for the lawn to use.

Then comes planting. Plant cool-season grasses during the cooler parts of the year, warm-season grasses once the weather stays dependably above 60° F. in spring or early summer. You may have the choice of sodding, sprigging or plugging, or seeding, depending on the grass species you have selected—not all grasses are available in all forms. Sodding has the fastest results: You virtually roll or lay out a ready-made lawn. Within four weeks of favorable weather, your lawn is established. Runoff and erosion during the extra watering necessary to establish a lawn are minimal with sod, making it ideal if you absolutely must have grass on a slope. Sod also helps smother potential weeds present in the freshly prepared soil. Unfortunately, fewer species are available as sod, especially bunch-forming types, for these cannot be harvested as solid pieces of living carpet.

Also, sod is more expensive and takes brute force to install. The rolls or squares are back-breakingly heavy.

Seeding offers a greater choice of grass species at a much cheaper price and is easy to do, but it requires a great deal more vigilance until the grass is established, about two months if everything goes well. Be sure to select high-quality seed for good germination and less contamination by weeds and undesirable grasses. You need to protect the young lawn from all traffic, water frequently but gently and watch for and hoe the inevitable opportunistic weeds that are always a problem unless you use chemical controls. Ideally you should prepare the seedbed several weeks ahead and water it, to make most of the dormant weed seeds sprout, which you then remove before you apply the grass seed. Laying a mesh cloth or a fine layer of straw over the freshly sown seed helps retain moisture and shade the tender, developing shoots. Remove this protective cover once the grass is 1 inch tall, and keep it lightly moist with frequent, gentle waterings until it reaches 3 inches; then christen it with its first mowing.

Sprigging and plugging falls between seeding and sodding in terms of advantages and disadvantages. Here you plant small sprigs or plugs of grass at the recommended spacing.

An established lawn should be watered only when needed. A lawn asks for water when it does not perk back up minutes after being walked on. Grasses that are naturally a bright green turn a darker, almost blue-black, shadowy shade when thirsty. Gray-green grasses become more gray. If only small areas of lawn seem dry due to differences in soil or a spotty watering system, water these by hand rather than wasting water by irrigating the whole lawn.

Most grass species do better when mowed taller than recommended, especially during the times of the year that don't favor rapid growth. A taller blade grows deeper roots and shades them, cooling them and reducing evaporation, thus conserving water and reducing plant stress. The less a lawn is stressed, the fewer problems you will have with insects and disease. A taller, thicker grass shades out weeds. Mow high and often; never remove more than 30 percent of the leaf blade at one time. Keep your mower blade sharp to reduce injury and stress; ragged cuts lose more water to transpiration than clean ones.

Leave mower clippings on the grass; they will break down quickly, recycling nutrients and organic matter back to the lawn. Contrary to popular belief, fallen clippings do not cause thatch. Thatch is a buildup of dead grass that results from a sterile soil with no decomposing organisms in it. Thatch harbors harmful insects and makes water and air penetration difficult. By limiting applications of inorganic fertilizers, fungicides and pesticides, you can bring the soil back to life and help reduce thatch. Until then, you need to remove it mechanically with a dethatching rake or machine.

To keep a heavily used lawn from suffocating and declining due to trampling and compaction or excessive thatch buildup, consider renting a core-aerating machine once or twice a year, during active growth. These machines bore out plugs of soil and grass quickly and easily, generally at 3-inch intervals and a similar depth, leaving small holes for air, water and fertilizer to penetrate. Water the turf a day or two before you aerate to make the job easier on you and the machine, and water again once you have finished. A good plan is to topdress the lawn with a slow-release fertilizer or ¼ to ½ inch of fine compost right after aerating, and then water again.

Many species of grass appreciate some fertilizer, especially a bit of extra nitrogen. Slow-release organic lawn fertilizers are more expensive but longer-lasting than cheaper inorganic formulations. The latter are easily lost to leaching; the grass is able to use only a small portion of the nitrogen and must do so quickly, resulting in uneven spurts of lush, lanky top growth. Fertilizer runoff has been broadly implicated in water contamination and the demise of aquatic life. Apply it with caution, if at all. Cool-season grasses need a feeding in early autumn and perhaps a smaller dose again in early spring when growth resumes. Heavy-feeding, warm-season grasses such as Bermuda grass need smaller, more frequent doses throughout their growing season. The native species need little, if any, additional fertilizer at all.

In two years, this waterwise planting of Penstemon strictus and lamb's ear has filled in, crowding out weeds and reducing evaporation from the soil.

MAINTENANCE OF THE WATERWISE GARDEN

If the waterwise garden has yet to prove itself to you, it promises to do so in the realm of ongoing care. After the first busy year, when weeds are at their worst and water needs of unestablished plants run high, a waterwise garden promises to require less tedious maintenance and artificial intervention, be it fertilizer, pesticide, pruner or mower, than a traditional landscape of similar size and scope. Drought-adapted plants are less likely to suffer stress that invites insects and diseases. They grow more slowly than lush water guzzlers, so mowing, trimming and pruning are needed less frequently. And, the less you mow and prune, the less you force new growth that requires you to mow and prune once again. If you have chosen a naturalistic style for your waterwise design, you will find yourself called upon for minimal primping. Seedheads are allowed to form, gracing the dormant garden with their interesting shapes, textures and sounds in the wind, and their bounty is spread for the coming years.

Weeding chores are diminished in a waterwise garden, thanks to good irrigation practices, the use of mulch and thrift about watering in general. Once plants fill in, you may actually have to look hard to find a weed. Keep an eye out for them nevertheless, for they steal needed moisture from desirable plants.

If you do find it necessary to fertilize, as in the case of soil that lacks a vital nutrient or the particular need of a certain plant, be careful not to overapply, for plants that are watered less often can burn easily as there is less water to flush out the excess fertilizer. An added problem is the salt accumulation common in dry soils that are overfertilized and not leached out by water. Besides, many drought-tolerant plants thrive in nutrient-poor soils, and actually suffer from too much nitrogen or organic matter. Overfed plants grow too quickly, resulting in higher susceptibility to disease, insect attack and stress. They also require more water. Don't push your plants with extra food; it will backfire. Enjoy the easy-care harmony that exists in your waterwise garden. A plant that doesn't need your intervention to do well is a happy, healthy plant.

PLANT PORTRAITS

It would seem impossible to do a comprehensive job of recommending waterwise plants to North American gardeners, for our climates and conditions vary so much across this vast continent. Until genetic engineering presents us with the perfect, completely adaptable, waterwise plant (and I'm not sure we'd want such a thing), educated trial and error remains the best way to select plants for our gardens.

The following plant portraits and lists for woody plants are organized in five climatic regions. The cold, humid region—the Northeast and Midwest—experiences enough natural rainfall to support a good number of trees, both native and exotic, without extra irrigation. The air is more humid. Temperatures can be extreme, with very cold winters—minimums ranging from about 10° F. down to –50° F.—and often hot summers, which is when periodic droughts occur and waterwise plants play an important role. The cold, dry region is characterized by low humidity and little rainfall; often a large proportion of this limited annual precipitation falls as snow during the dormant season. Winters are bitter, with similar ranges as the cold, humid region, and summers can be very hot. Included here are the Great Plains, the Rocky Mountains and the Great Basin. The hot, humid region has intensely hot, muggy summers and less severe winters, rarely below 10° F. Rainfall may be ample one year, then periodic drought may occur during the hottest times of the year the next. Most parts of the southern states and the eastern half of Texas have this type of climate. The hot, dry region receives little natural rainfall and has extremely low humidity, intense summer heat and mild winter temperatures. The lower altitudes of the Southwest, inland southern California and southwestern Texas fall into this category. The last region, mild maritime, is characterized by an absence of extreme temperatures—neither very hot nor cold. Considerable drought may occur, especially during the summer, although along the coast there may be high atmospheric humidity. Often called a Mediterranean climate, it describes most of the Pacific coastal region, with central and southern California coasts in most need of waterwise plants.

If you look closely at the lists, you will see plants repeated in more than one region, for many have a wide range of adaptability. In each plant portrait, other regions where the plant might thrive are also mentioned. If you live in a region that shares characteristics with more than one of the artificial divisions used here— for example, you live inland in north-central California (mild maritime and hot, dry), or in a coastal mid-Atlantic state (cold and hot, humid and some mild maritime), the high altitudes of the Southwest (cold and hot, dry) or the southern Midwest (cold and hot, humid)—you will want to look at the plants suggested for more than one region. There is a tremendous amount of potential overlap; plants don't fall neatly into categories, which while making it more difficult to write this book, is actually a blessing. Gardening is a wonderfully inexact science, with boundless opportunity to experiment and play. And if a plant doesn't thrive, we can absolve

In early spring, the emerging foliage of striped bulbous oat grass carpets the ground beneath flowering quince, a tough old-fashioned shrub that needs little water.

ourselves and conveniently blame Mother Nature. For herbaceous plants—perennials, groundcovers and annuals—the five regional divisions are less useful, for these plants are widely adaptable, and so the regional divisions have been omitted altogether.

Each region includes plant portraits for 9 outstanding water-wise plants: 8 trees and shrubs, and 1 vine. Lists of additional waterwise plants for each region follow. When choosing a plant for your garden, keep in mind what you want, how much space is available and what the site's conditions are. A happy balance among these parameters makes for both a happy plant and a happy gardener. Be aware that some attractive introduced species are very adaptable and may become weedy. For example, tree of heaven, Russian olive, Chinaberry, Brazilian pepper tree and several of the brooms have made themselves a bit too comfortable in some regions. Such plants are marked with a "W" in the lists. If you live in an area where one of these species is troublesome, plant other species. When only a genus is given in the lists, this means that more than one species exists and that these are also waterwise.

PLANT PORTRAIT KEY

Here is a guide to the symbols and terms used throughout this section.

Latin name of the plant is in boldface italic.

Phonetic pronunciation of the Latin name is in parentheses. There is often more than one way to pronounce any Latin name. The only way to pronounce names incorrectly is not to follow the sequence of syllables.

Common name of the plant is in boldface type. Often there is more than one common name.

Native American identifies those plants growing in North America at the time of its colonization.

Season of bloom: SP = spring, SU = summer, F = fall, W = winter; E = early, L = late, *e.g.* ESP = early spring.

The average hours of sun needed per day is indicated by symbols. The first symbol is what the plant prefers, but it is adaptable to all conditions listed. The amount of sun needed by a plant may change depending on the amount of moisture available; more moisture allows some plants to tolerate more sun. Altitude too affects sun and shade. High-altitude sun is fiercer, and many plants that love sun at sea level prefer afternoon shade on the high plains or in the mountains. Finally, latitude can be a determining factor. Full sun in the South is more intense than it is in the North.

○*Sun*—Six hours or longer of direct sunlight per day.

◑*Part Shade*—Three to six hours of direct sunlight per day.

Symbols for:
✿ Fragrant blossoms or foliage
⚱ Long-lasting cut flower
❀ Long bloomer—a month or longer
↗ Suitable for drying

Size: The average range of height and width are given for each plant at maturity. Soil, moisture and climate variations may cause a plant to grow a bit larger or remain somewhat smaller than these averages.

HOT, DRY CLIMATES

No cacti or succulents are included; these make excellent accent plants, but be aware that the majority of larger specimens are dug from the wild, often by so-called cactus rustlers. Some may be legitimately salvaged, but will still be difficult to establish in the garden with any dependable success. These larger plants include many species of columnar cacti, ocotillo and yucca.

If you are afflicted with the notorious southwestern caliche, dig a 5-foot-wide, 3- to 5-foot-deep hole (or whatever necessary to penetrate the caliche); plant on a tight mound of soil so the plant won't settle too deeply.

Waterwise Trees for Hot, Dry Climates

Ceratonia siliqua (se-ra-TO-nee-a si-LI-kwa) **carob tree, St. John's bread,** Mediterranean, also grows well in mild, maritime climates. ○
Size: 30 to 40 feet tall and wide
Flower Color: Insignificant
Water: Prefers little to none once established.
Characteristics: Carob tree is a densely rounded, lush, evergreen tree. It tends to be multi-stemmed but can easily be trained to a single stem. Dark green, shiny, leathery compound leaves, up to 1 foot in length, are made up of several 2- to 4-inch leaflets. Small rose-red flower clusters appear in spring; male flowers have a strong scent. Female trees bear long, 6- to 8-inch, dark brown pods in fall, from which a sweet, chocolatelike pulp can be extracted. Carob tree resists oak root fungus, tolerates wind and heat, and is cold-hardy to at least 18° F. once established. It is very fire-retardant and also good for erosion control. 'Cal Poly' is a fruitless cultivar.
Cultural Information: Do not water frequently or shallowly—promotes Texas root rot and shallow root systems that can damage driveways and sidewalks. For fruit to form, plant both male and female trees. May need to prune lower branches for form.

Cercidium (sur-SI-dee-um) **palo verde,** some Native American, some Mexican, also grows in warmer parts of mild, maritime climates, SP, ESU. ○
Size: 15 to 25 feet, depending on species
Flower Color: Yellow
Water: None necessary once established, although responsive thereafter to occasional deep watering.
Characteristics: Palo verdes are deciduous, fine-textured trees native to the deserts of the Southwest and Mexico. Their small compound leaves are absent most of the year, leaving a pretty tracery of green or blue-green twigs. All have showy green bark, hence the Spanish common name, and bloom profusely in spring. The dense branching provides some shade even without leaves. Palo verdes are not known for their neatness, for they drop flowers, leaves and small dry seedpods. The pealike yellow flowers attract hummingbirds.

Cercidium floridum, blue palo verde, is a fast-growing native tree to 25 to 30 feet tall and often wider than that. It casts good shade. This tree usually is multiple-trunked, and the thorny, blue-green branches may droop to the ground. In mid-spring, blue palo verde is covered in 2- to 4-inch racemes of golden flowers for two weeks. It is hardy to 0° to 10° F. *C. microphyllum,* called foothills palo verde for its native habitat, is smaller—to 20 feet tall—and slower growing than blue palo verde. The foliage and bark are more yellow-green, the branches and form stiffer and more upright. Overall, it has a rounded form. It blooms a little later than blue palo verde, with paler yellow flowers, for several weeks. Foothills palo verde is the toughest, tolerating caliche soils and complete drought. *C. praecox,* Sonoran palo verde, has the best treelike form of all the species yet is thornier and less hardy, only to 20° F. 'Desert Museum', ✿ a bigeneric hybrid between *Cercidium* and *Parkinsonia,* is a superior single-trunked tree, 15 to 25 feet tall, fast-growing, with upright branching and lacking thorns. It is also quite hardy. The large, brilliant yellow flowers are lightly fragrant and borne for more than a month.
Cultural Information: Palo verdes are resistant to Texas root rot and thrive in heat. Avoid heavy pruning, for they heal poorly.

Cercidium floridum

Ceratonia siliqua

Cupressus glabra (ku-PRE-sus GLAY-bra) **smooth Arizona cypress,** Native American. ○ 🐢

Size: 30 to 60 feet tall, 20 to 40 feet wide

Flower Color: Insignificant

Water: None, or occasional deep waterings once established.

Characteristics: Smooth Arizona cypress is a fast-growing evergreen tree native to central Arizona. Upright and pyramidal when young, it becomes more irregular and open with age. The smooth red bark contrasts nicely with its threadlike, aromatic gray-green foliage. Selections with more silver foliage ('Gareei'), and smaller, more formal habit ('Pyramidalis') are available. *C. arizonica* is closely related but not as attractive as it lacks the lovely bark characteristic of this species. Smooth Arizona cypress is a tough tree, resistant to cypress canker, tolerant of alkaline soil and hardy to −20° F. It thrives in heat and makes an excellent windbreak.

Cultural Information: Any well-drained soil will do. Good air circulation helps prevent spider mites.

ADDITIONAL WATERWISE TREES FOR HOT, DRY CLIMATES

Acacia W (see tree portrait, page 69) 🐢

Bauhinia congesta Anacacho orchid tree

Brahea armata blue fan palm

Casuarina beefwood, she oak

Celtis hackberry ◖

Chilopsis linearis desert willow 🐢

Cordia boissieri anacahuita, Texas olive

Dalea spinosa smoke tree 🐢

Eucalyptus gum—many are waterwise W 🐢

Ficus carica common fruiting fig ◖

Fraxinus ornus flowering ash 🐢

Leucaena retusa golden ball tree 🐢

Lysiloma microphylla v. *thornberi* feather tree

Melaleuca paperbark, bottlebrush (see tree portrait, page 70) 🐢

Melia azedarach 'Umbraculiformis' Texas umbrella tree W 🐢

Olea europaea 'Swan Hill' olive

Olneya tesota ironwood

Parkinsonia aculeata retama, Mexican palo verde W 🐢

Pinus aristata bristlecone pine

Pinus edulis pinyon pine

Pinus eldarica Afghan, Mondell pine

Pinus halepensis aleppo pine

Pistacia pistache (see tree portrait, page 56)

Prosopis mesquite W 🐢

Rhus lancea African sumac

Robinia × ambigua 'Idahoensis' Idaho locust (see tree portrait, page 60) 🐢

Sapindus soapberry

Sophora secundiflora Texas mountain laurel, mescal bean (see shrub portrait, page 53) 🐢

Ungnadia speciosa Mexican buckeye 🐢

Vitex agnus-castus chaste tree, monk's pepper tree ◖ (see tree portrait, page 56) 🐢

Washingtonia filifera California fan palm

Waterwise Shrubs for Hot, Dry Climates

Caesalpinia (say-sal-PI-nee-a) **bird of paradise bush,** native of tropical Mexico, South America, West Indies, can be grown in hot, humid climates as well, SP, SU, F. ○ ✿

Size: 5 to 10 feet tall and wide

Flower Colors: Yellow, orange, red

Water: Best with occasional deep watering, especially when flowering.

Characteristics: Bird of paradise bushes are fast-growing, tropical-looking shrubs with feathery, fine-textured compound leaves, deciduous in all but the very warmest climates. Their flowers are showy, with five petals and long, protruding stamens. They thrive in heat. The fruit is poisonous. Hummingbirds visit the flowers. *Caesalpinia gilliesii,* yellow bird of paradise bush, is the hardiest, with an open, unbranched vertical growth habit. It blooms all summer in clusters of yellow flowers with long, red, 4- to 5-inch stamens. Yellow bird of paradise bush has naturalized in the Southwest; it is hardy to at least 10° F. *C. mexicana* is a larger, coarser shrub with lemon-yellow flowers from spring to fall. It dies down to the ground at 30° F., yet is hardy to about 20°, coming back strongly like a herbaceous perennial. *C. pulcherrima,* Barbados pride, blooms all spring, summer and fall with orange to red flowers. It has hardiness similar to that of *C. mexicana.*

Cupressus glabra 'Blue Ice'

Caesalpinia gilliesii

Cultural Information: Any soil will do as long as it is well-drained. Susceptible to Texas root rot if overwatered. If cold weather doesn't prune them to the ground, you can do the same to keep them compact, neat and vigorous.

Calliandra eriophylla

(ka-li-AN-dra e-ri-o-FI-la) **fairy duster,** Native American, also good in warmer parts of mild maritime climates, SU. ○
Size: 3 feet tall and wide
Flower Colors: Pink, white
Water: Best with occasional deep watering.
Characteristics: Fairy duster is a small, fine-textured, airy shrub native to the Southwest. Its compound ferny leaves are semievergreen, dropping in extreme drought or cold. Fluffy 1- to 2-inch pink or white flower clusters in summer, favored by hummingbirds. Fairy duster is hardy to about 15° F., sometimes lower. Deep pink selections are available. *C. californica,* the Baja fairy duster, is similar but a foot or so larger and with bright red powderpuff flowers that last longer, well into autumn. It is less hardy, only to 28° F.
Cultural Information: Fairy dusters require a well-drained soil.

Leucophyllum (loo-ko-FI-lum) **Texas ranger, Texas sage, ceniza,** Native American, LSU, F. ○
Size: Varies with species
Flower Colors: Pink, lavender, purple, white
Water: None, or occasional deep watering once established.

Characteristics: All cenizas are hardy to 10° F., some lower. These shrubs are native to the deserts of the Southwest and northern Mexico, reveling in heat and tolerating strong winds. They have dense evergreen foliage that becomes almost succulent with moisture and is generally covered in gray or silver hairs, hence the Spanish common name ceniza, ash-gray. Showy, 1-inch snapdragonlike flowers appear in late summer and fall, responding to irrigation or rains, and are visited by hummingbirds. *L. frutescens* is the most commonly grown species, a rounded evergreen shrub that grows to 8 feet tall and wide. Softly fuzzy gray foliage sets off violet flowers. 'Green Cloud' has sage-green foliage and larger, rose-purple flowers; 'White Cloud' has gray foliage and large white flowers; 'Convent' has brilliant magenta flowers and silver leaves; and the variety *compactum* is only 3 feet tall and wide. *L. candidum,* silver-leaf sage, is shorter at 4 feet tall and wide, and has dark violet flowers and very silver foliage. *L. laevigatum,* Chihuahuan rain sage, has green leaves and grows 4 feet tall and a bit wider, with a more open habit than other cenizas. Lavender-blue flowers bloom more often throughout the summer and fall than other species. *L. minus,* called Big Bend silverleaf, is the toughest and hardiest, and grows to only 3 feet tall and wide. It has silver leaves and lavender blossoms. Cultivars 'Silver Cloud', with deep purple flowers and almost

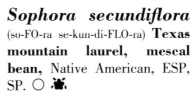

Calliandra californica

white foliage, and the similar 'Thundercloud' are choice shrubs. 'Raincloud' is a vigorous hybrid between *L. minus* and *L. frutescens,* with electric blue-violet flowers. *L. zygophyllum,* blue rain sage, has gray-green leaves and reaches 6 feet tall and wide. It is very dense and rounded, with purple-blue flowers. 'Blue Ranger' is a good selection.
Cultural Information: Cenizas can be pruned to shape as desired, even into hedges. They prefer a well-drained, alkaline soil and are susceptible to Texas root rot if overwatered.

Sophora secundiflora

(so-FO-ra se-kun-di-FLO-ra) **Texas mountain laurel, mescal bean,** Native American, ESP, SP. ○ 🐾
Size: 15 feet tall, 10 feet wide
Flower Color: Purple
Water: Occasional deep watering, or none once established.
Characteristics: This large evergreen shrub is native to the Southwest. Pinnately compound leaves of 1- to 2-inch dark green, shiny leaflets form a lush canopy. Profuse 6-inch

Leucophyllum frutescens

Sophora secundiflora

Vauquelinia

clusters of grape-scented, 1-inch purple flowers appear in early spring. Gray woody pods open to show bright red, poisonous seeds. Texas mountain laurel grows slowly and is hardy to 10° F. It thrives in heat and can be grown on slopes. A somewhat rare white-flowered form exists. Bees frequent the flowers. *S. gypsophila* v. *guadalupensis*, Guadalupe mountain laurel, is only 3 to 4 feet tall, but three times as wide, with larger flowers and silvery leaves.

Cultural Information: Alkaline, well-drained soil is ideal. Can be pruned and trained into a small tree, or to make a more compact, bushy shrub. Dislikes transplanting.

Vauquelinia (vaw-ke-LI-nee-a) **Arizona or Chisos rosewood,** Native American, LSP, ESU. ○ 🐢

Size: 15 feet tall, 10 feet wide
Flower Color: White
Water: None, or occasional deep watering once established.
Characteristics: Two species, *V. californica* and *V. angustifolia*, are very similar. The first is native to Arizona, the other, with narrower foliage, to desert regions of Texas. Both are dense, upright evergreen shrubs and somewhat slow growing. Narrow, dark green, leathery foliage reminiscent of that of oleander sets off the white flower clusters at the branch tips, and turns somewhat bronze in cold temperatures. The bark is a warm reddish brown. Both species are hardy to at least 15° F., tolerate strong wind, like heat and do well on slopes.

Cultural Information: Well-drained soil is preferred. Good air circulation helps fend off red spider mites.

ADDITIONAL WATERWISE SHRUBS FOR HOT, DRY CLIMATES

Acacia W 🐢
Aloysia bee bush, oreganillo 🐢
Anisacanthus desert honeysuckle, flame acanthus
Atriplex saltbush
Baccharis sarothroides 'Centennial' desert broom
Bouvardia ◐
Buddleya marrubiifolia woolly butterfly bush (see shrub portrait, page 57)
Cassia feathery senna
Ceratoides (Eurotia) lanata winterfat
Cercocarpus mountain mahogany, palo duro (see shrub portrait, page 60)
Chamaebatiaria millefolium fernbush 🐢
Chrysothamnus nauseosus rabbitbrush, chamisa
Cordia cordia, wild olive
Cowania mexicana cliff rose 🐢
Dalea dalea 🐢
Dodonaea viscosa hop bush
Encelia farinosa brittle bush
Ephedra joint fir
Fallugia paradoxa Apache plume (see shrub portrait, page 61)
Fendlera rupicola cliff fendler bush 🐢
Forestiera neomexicana New Mexico privet
Fouquieria ocotillo, buggy whip, boojum
Fremontodendron flannel bush
Isomeris arborea bladder bush
Juniperus juniper 🐢

Justicia (Beloperone) californica chuparosa
Lantana camara lantana W 🐢
Larrea tridentata creosote bush, hediondilla 🐢
Lavandula lavender 🐢
Leptodactylon prickly phlox
Mahonia fremontii, M. haematocarpa mahonia 🐢
Nerium oleander oleander 🐢
Parthenium guayule, mariola
Pavonia lasiopetala Texas rock rose, rose mallow
Rhus sumac, lemita ◐ (see shrub portrait, page 66) 🐢
Salvia (see perennial portrait, page 79) 🐢
Santolina lavender cotton 🐢
Simmondsia chinensis goatnut
Spartium junceum Spanish broom W 🐢
Syringa laciniata (see shrub portrait, page 62) 🐢
Syringa × persica (see shrub portrait, page 63) 🐢
Tecoma stans var. *angustata* esperanza, yellow bells

Waterwise Vines for Hot, Dry Climates

Macfadyena unguiscati (mak-FAD-ye-na UN-gwis-KA-ti) **cat's claw vine, yellow trumpet vine,** Mexico and Central America, will also grow in mild, maritime climates, ESP. ○ ◐

Size: 30 to 40 feet
Flower Color: Yellow
Water: None necessary once established.
Characteristics: Cat's claw vine is an aggressive vine evergreen to about 20° F. Its shiny green leaves are made of two leaflets and three clawlike tendrils, hence its common name. The

foliage takes on purple tints in cold temperatures. The vine is hardy to about 10° F. Showy yellow, 2-inch trumpets bloom in early spring. Cat's claw vine can climb on any surface. It prefers hot weather, reveling on hot surfaces, and can tolerate wind. *Cultural Information:* Most soils are satisfactory. Prune hard after bloom to keep in bounds.

ADDITIONAL WATERWISE VINES FOR HOT, DRY CLIMATES

Campsis grandiflora Chinese trumpet vine (see vine portrait, page 59)
Lathyrus latifolius perennial pea vine (see vine portrait, page 63)

Macfadyena unguis-cati

HOT, HUMID CLIMATES

Waterwise Trees for Hot, Humid Climates

Cercis canadensis var. *mexicana* (SUR-sis ka-na-DEN-sis me-xi-KA-na) **Mexican redbud**, Native American, will also grow in hot, dry climates with more water, ESP. ○ ◑

Size: 8 to 12 feet tall, 6 to 8 feet wide
Flower Color: Pink
Water: Occasional deep watering once established.
Characteristics: This lovely small tree is a close relative of the eastern and western redbuds but is native to Texas and Mexico, and has greater tolerance for intense heat and drought. The foliage is the loveliest of the group—glossy, heart-shaped, rich green and waxy, with undulating margins. It blooms before leafing out, as do the others, in tight clusters of small pea-shaped flowers all along the branches. The flowers are a paler pink than most redbuds. Mexican redbud can be trained as a single or multi-stemmed specimen. It is hardy to 0° F., with some variability depending on seed source. Fall foliage color is yellow. *C. canadensis* var. *texensis*, sometimes *C. reniformis*, Texas redbud, is closely related, also with glossy foliage. 'White Texas' has white flowers; 'Oklahoma', bright rose flowers.

Cultural Information: Any well-drained soil will do. Good air circulation helps ward off pests and diseases that sometimes trouble the redbuds.

Ginkgo biloba (GING-ko bi-LO-ba) **maidenhair tree, ginkgo**, China, grows in all but the hottest climates. ○

Size: 50 to 100 feet tall, shape varies from columnar to broad
Flower Color: Insignificant
Water: Occasional deep watering is appreciated, especially when young; needs extra water in dry climates.
Characteristics: Ginkgo is a long-lived deciduous tree of great grace and dignity. It is one of the most ancient species, known to have thrived during the early years of the dinosaurs. Unusual fan-shaped leaves turn a fabulous golden color in autumn. Avoid female trees, for their messy fruit has a rotten odor. Ginkgo tolerates wind and seaside conditions. Hardy to at least −30° F. Cultivars: 'Autumn Gold', 'Palo Alto', 'Santa Cruz', all males with broadly oval crowns; 'Fairmount' more formal in shape; 'Princeton Sentry', male with narrow columnar shape; 'Lakefield', 'Mayfield' and 'Saratoga', smaller, pyramidal males.
Cultural Information: Prefers a well-drained soil.

Cercis canadensis texensis

Ginkgo biloba

Pistacia chinensis (pis-TA-shi-a si-NEN-sis) **Chinese pistache,** China, also does well in mild, maritime and hot, dry climates. ○
Size: 30 to 50 feet tall and wide
Flower Color: Insignificant
Water: Best with occasional deep waterings.
Characteristics: Chinese pistache is an attractive, deciduous shade tree with a rounded crown. Its lush, dark green, 8-inch pinnate (compound, with leaflets arranged along an axis, like a feather) leaves turn bright orange-red in autumn. Female trees bear small red fruit that ripens to blue. Chinese pistache is resistant to oak root fungus, tolerates wind and is hardy to at least 10° F. Cultivar 'Keith Davey' has an

Pistachia chinensis

especially good, dense, rounded form.
Cultural Information: Best in well-drained soil, to protect against verticillium wilt and Texas root rot.

Vitex agnus-castus (VY-tex AN-yus-KAS-tus) **chaste tree, monk's pepper,** Mediterranean, also does well in warmer parts of mild, maritime climates, and in hot, dry climates, SU, LSU. ○ 🐢
Size: 15 feet tall and wide
Flower Colors: Lavender-blue, white, pink
Water: Occasional deep watering helps it grow to tree proportions; without water, remains a shrub.
Characteristics: This multi-trunked small tree offers long-blooming spikes of fragrant flowers in summer. Deciduous foliage, also fragrant, is deeply cut, palmate, like a marijuana leaf. Chaste tree has an open habit. In colder regions it dies down to the ground and is effective as a large herbaceous perennial or shrub. Butterflies and hummingbirds both appreciate the flowers. It is susceptible to Texas root rot but resistant to oak root fungus. Hardy above ground to 10° F, roots to about −20° F. Cultivars: 'Latifolia' has wider foliage and is supposedly a bit hardier; 'Alba' and 'Silver Spire' have white flowers; 'Rosea' has pink flowers. *V. negundo* is very similar, with more gray-green foliage; its cultivar 'Heterophylla' has pretty, finely toothed, feathery leaves.
Cultural Information: A well-drained soil keeps root rot at bay.

ADDITIONAL WATERWISE TREES FOR HOT, HUMID CLIMATES

Albizia julibrissin hardy silk tree W 🐢

Aralia elata angelica tree ◑

Carya hickory

Catalpa bignonioides southern catalpa 🐢

Cedrus cedar

Celtis hackberry ◑

× *Cupressocyparis leylandii* Leyland cypress

Diospyros kaki, D. virginiana persimmon

Eriobotrya japonica loquat 🐢

Fraxinus ornus flowering ash 🐢

Gymnocladus dioicas Kentucky coffee tree

Ilex vomitoria yaupon ◑

Juglans nigra black walnut

Koelreuteria bipinnata, K. paniculata goldenrain tree

Lagerstroemia indica crape myrtle

Maclura pomifera Osage orange W

Melaleuca paperbark, bottlebrush (see tree portrait, page 70)

Melia azedarach Texas umbrella tree, Chinaberry W 🐢

Pinus many pines

Ptelea trifoliata water ash, hop tree ◑

Pterocarya fraxinifolia wingnut

Quercus oak

Sapindus soapberry

Sophora japonica Japanese pagoda tree, scholar tree 🐢

Taxodium distichum bald cypress loves swamps yet is drought-tolerant

Ulmus parvifolia lacebark elm (see tree portrait, page 65)

Viburnum prunifolium blackhaw

Vitex agnus-castus

Waterwise Shrubs for Hot, Humid Climates

Buddleia (**sometimes spelled *Buddleya***) (BUD-lee-ya) **butterfly bush,** China, one Native American, also good in all other climates except where cold hardiness is a problem, ESU, SU, LSU, F. ○ 🦋 ❀

Size: Depends on species
Flower Colors: Purple, lavender, rose, orange, white
Water: Best with occasional deep watering.
Characteristics: Fast-growing, semideciduous shrubs, often look best when severely pruned during the dormant season. Most butterfly bushes tolerate strong wind and seaside conditions. Long-blooming flowers attract hordes of butterflies and sometimes hummingbirds as well. Deer avoid these shrubs. *B. alternifolia* is a large, fine-textured wild fountain of a shrub, 15 feet tall and wide, with narrow, gray-green, willowlike foliage on arching stems. It blooms the earliest, in late spring or early summer, covering its branches with pale lavender flower clusters. This is the hardiest butterfly bush, to at least −15° F. The cultivar 'Argentea' has especially silver foliage. *B. crispa* ❀ grows to 15 feet and has whitish, felted leaves. Pendulous clusters of pale lavender flowers emerge from furry white buds. Not hardy below 20° F. *B. davidii,* ❀ called summer lilac, has long, pointed, oval leaves with white undersides. It is generally 5 to 10 feet tall and wide, and blooms for two months in summer. The long 6- to 12-inch

flower spikes are richly fragrant. Summer lilac is hardy to about −10° F., but dies to the ground at less severe temperatures. It is so vigorous that cutting it to the ground each winter helps its appearance. Numerous cultivars exist, including 'Black Knight', a deep purple; 'Royal Red', deep wine-red; 'White Profusion', white; and 'Nanho Blue' and 'Nanho Purple', smaller shrubs with daintier flower spikes, finer-textured stems and smaller, more silvery foliage. *Buddleia* × 'Golden Glow' and 'Sungold' have smaller flower spikes in amber tones and are not quite as hardy as *B. davidii*. *B. marrubiifolia*, woolly butterfly bush, is a 5-foot native to Texas. Its semievergreen, woolly, whitish-tawny rounded foliage is aromatic, as are the golden-orange flowers in dense 1-inch balls. It is the most drought-tolerant butterfly bush and hardy to 15° F.
Cultural Information: A deep, well-drained soil is best. Good air circulation helps prevent spider mite infestations.

Cotinus (ko-TY-nus) smoke-bush,

will grow in all but the very coldest climates, LSP, SU, F. ○
Size: 8 to 30 feet tall and a little narrower, depending on species
Flower Colors: Purple, peach, rose, buff (flower stalks)
Water: None, or occasional deep watering once established.
Characteristics: Smokebushes are large deciduous shrubs with rounded leaves that emerge peach, turning a glaucous blue-green. Fall color can

Buddleia alternifolia

Buddleia davidii

be phenomenal. Peach, pink, purple and buff fluffy fruit stalks look like smoke, giving the plants their common name. Deer avoid them. They are resistant to oak root fungus. *C. coggygria*, from central and southern Europe, is 8 to 15 feet tall and not quite as wide. Fall color is not as dependable as with the next species. Purple foliage cultivars 'Velvet Cloak' and 'Royal Purple' are showy additions to the garden, with purple and rosy bronze "smoke puffs." Hardy to about −10° F. *C. obovatus (C. americanus)* is a large shrub or small tree, growing 15 to 30 feet tall and 10 to 15 feet wide. Native to southern states, it has attractive, light gray bark, tawny-peach "smoke puffs" and fantastic, dependably orange, rose and red fall color. American smokebush is hardier than *C. coggygria*, to about −30° F., and prefers slightly alkaline soil.
Cultural Information: Can be pruned hard for shape and, on the purple-leaved cultivars, to force vigorous new growth with more intense purple color. Well-drained soil is preferred.

Cotinus coggygria

Hibiscus syriacus
'Blue Bird'

Hibiscus syriacus (hy-BIS-kus si-ri-AK-us) **rose of Sharon,** China, will grow in all but the coldest climates, ESU, SU, LSU. ○ ◑ ✿

Size: 8 to 12 feet tall, 6 to 10 feet wide
Flower Colors: Lilac, rose, pink, white, bicolor
Water: Occasional deep watering is appreciated.
Characteristics: Rose of Sharon is a tough, deciduous, old-fashioned shrub or small tree, vase-shaped, with lobed green foliage. It is grown for its abundant display of large, 3- to 5-inch tropical-looking flowers, single or double and with or without contrasting dark eye. The flowers bloom in late summer and often continue into the fall, attracting hummingbirds. Rose of Sharon is resistant to oak root fungus. Japanese beetles can be a problem. It is hardy to about −15° F. Many cultivars exist; a few of the best are: 'Diana', pure white single; 'Blue Bird', lavender-blue single with purple eye; 'Collie Mullens' and 'Lucy', double rose; 'Lady Stanley', double pale pink with red eye; 'Helene', blush white single with pink eye; 'Red Heart', single white with red eye; 'Woodbridge', rose-red single.
Cultural Information: Prune hard during the dormant season, leaving only a few buds on the previous year's growth, for better and larger blooms. Needs a well-drained soil.

Lespedeza thunbergii (les-pe-DEE-za thun-BER-ji-eye) **bush clover,** China and Japan, LSU, F. ○

Size: 4 to 6 feet tall and a bit wider
Flower Colors: Rose, white
Water: Occasional deep watering.
Characteristics: This fine-textured, graceful shrub has arching, sparsely branched stems smothered in flowers in late summer and autumn. Dainty cloverlike, blue-green leaves clothe the branches. The pea-shaped flowers form dense clusters along the top 2 to 3 feet of branches. Bush clover dies to the ground at about 10° F, coming back like a herbaceous perennial. It is root-hardy to about −15° F. 'White Fountain' is a lovely white-flowered form; 'Pink Fountain' has clear pink flowers without the purple tints of the species; 'Gibraltar' is especially floriferous.
Cultural Information: Thrives in a deep, well-drained soil. Cut one-third of the branches back to the ground each dormant season, if cold weather hasn't done it for you, to invigorate the bush.

ADDITIONAL WATERWISE SHRUBS FOR HOT, HUMID CLIMATES

Abelia ◑ 🐢
Aucuba japonica ◑
Berberis barberry 🐢
Caesalpinia bird of paradise bush (see shrub portrait, page 52)
Callicarpa beauty berry ◑
Caryopteris × *clandonensis* blue mist spirea 🐢
Chaenomeles flowering quince
Chimonanthus praecox wintersweet 🐢
Cytisus broom W 🐢
Euonymus ◑
Ilex cornuta Chinese holly
Jasminum jasmine ◑ 🐢
Ligustrum privet ◑ W 🐢
Mahonia bealei leatherleaf mahonia ◑ 🐢
Nandina domestica heavenly bamboo ◑
Nerium oleander oleander 🐢
Osmanthus ◑ 🐢
Philadelphus mock orange 🐢
Pittosporum ◑ 🐢
Podocarpus macrophyllus southern yew ◑
Poncirus trifoliata hardy orange 🐢
Punica granatum pomegranate
Raphiolepis Indian hawthorn ◑
Rhododendron alabamense Alabama azalea ◑ 🐢

Lespedeza thunbergii

Rhododendron atlanticum coastal azalea ◐ ✿

Rhododendron flammeum Oconee azalea ◐ ✿

Rhododendron periclymenoides (R. nudiflorum) pinxterbloom azalea ◐ ✿

Rhododendron prinophyllum (R. roseum) roseshell azalea ◐ ✿

Rhus sumac (see shrub portrait, page 66) ✿

Rosa alba, R. spinosissima Scotch rose, *R. × harisonii* Harison's yellow rose, *R. laevigata* Cherokee rose, *R. wichuraiana* memorial rose, *R. banksiae* Lady Banks rose (see shrub portraits, pages 61 and 68) ✿

Salvia some shrubby sages (see perennial portrait, page 79) ✿

Spiraea spirea

Syringa laciniata cut-leaf lilac (see shrub portrait, page 62) ✿

Syringa × persica lilac (see shrub portrait, page 63) ✿

Waterwise Vines for Hot, Humid Climates

Campsis grandiflora
(KAMP-sis gran-di-FLO-ra) **Chinese trumpet vine,** Korea, will also grow in hot, dry climates and mild maritime climates, SU, F. ○ ◐ ✿

Size: 20 feet

Flower Color: Apricot-red

Water: Avoid watering to keep it from becoming overly vigorous.

Characteristics: Chinese trumpet vine is the better-behaved cousin of rampant American native trumpet creeper (*C. radicans*), a beautiful vine better suited to colder and/or drier climates that will keep it in check. Chinese trumpet vine is clothed in lush, deep green, deciduous pinnate foliage and showy trusses of 3-inch tubular flowers for many weeks, lending it a tropical look. It climbs by twining stems and clinging aerial rootlets that can damage masonry. Two excellent hybrid

cultivars, *C. tagliabuana* 'Madame Galen', salmon red, and 'Crimson Trumpet', scarlet, are hardier. Chinese trumpet vine revels in heat and tolerates wind and seaside conditions. Hummingbirds love its flowers. *Cultural Information:* Chinese trumpet vine can be invasive by root suckers and layering, especially if overwatered. Cut back hard to a few buds each winter for better flowering. It tolerates almost any soil, and will do well in part shade although flowering will be diminished.

ADDITIONAL WATERWISE VINES FOR HOT, HUMID CLIMATES

Lathyrus latifolius perennial pea vine (see vine portrait, page 63)

Lonicera sempervirens trumpet honeysuckle, coral honeysuckle (see vine portrait, page 68)

Solanum jasminoides potato vine (see vine portrait, page 74) ◐

Wisteria

Campsis tagliabuana 'Madame Galen'

Catalpa speciosa

Crataegus ambigua

COLD, DRY CLIMATES

Waterwise Trees for Cold, Dry Climates

Catalpa speciosa
(ka-TAL-pa spee-si-O-sa) **Western or hardy catalpa,** Native American, does well in all other climates except the very hottest and coldest, LSP, ESU. ○

Size: 40 to 60 feet tall, 30 to 40 feet wide

Flower Color: White

Water: Occasional deep watering is appreciated.

Characteristics: Western catalpa is a fast-growing, surprisingly tropical-looking deciduous tree with an open crown. Bright green, foot-long, heart-shaped leaves add to the lush effect. Tubular, white 2-inch flowers with yellow or tan markings, visited by hummingbirds, are held in upright 6-inch clusters above the foliage in early summer. Flowers, leaves and long seedpods are not for the neat freak. Western catalpa is hardy to at least −30° F. Protect from

harsh winds; the leaves can be damaged. Variety *purpurea* has purple new growth.

Cultural Information: Catalpa prefers good drainage, which is especially helpful in hot weather when root rot can be a problem.

Crataegus ambigua
(kre-TEE-gus am-BIG-wa) **Russian hawthorn,** Russia, also grows in cold, humid climates, LSP, ESU. ○

Size: 15 to 25 feet tall and wide

Maackia amurensis

Robinia × ambiqua 'Idahoensis'

Cercocarpus ledifolius

Flower Color: White
Water: Best with occasional deep waterings.
Characteristics: Russian hawthorn has a dense, twiggy form, rounded to vase-shaped. The rugged, thorny branches give it a gnarled, mature, picturesque look at a young age. The deeply cut foliage is small, only about 2 inches, and a somewhat glossy dark green. Fall color can be a good burgundy red. Clusters of small white flowers, beloved of bees, become masses of small red fruit in late summer and fall that birds devour. Russian hawthorn is hardy to −40° F. or colder. It is the toughest and most drought-tolerant of the hawthorns.
Cultural Information: Any well-drained soil is fine. Good air circulation keeps pests at a minimum.

Maackia amurensis

(MA-kee-a a-mu-REN-sis) **Amur maackia,** China, also good in cold, humid climates, SU, LSU. ○ ◐ 🐝
Size: 20 to 40 feet tall, 30 to 40 feet wide
Flower Color: White
Water: Occasional deep watering is helpful.
Characteristics: Amur maackia is a small, slow-growing, fine-textured deciduous tree with a round crown. Its compound leaves are a good, rich green. White, hay-scented flowers bloom in erect 6- to 8-inch spikes. The bark has a bronze, almost metallic sheen. Amur maackia can take a fair amount of wind.
Cultural Information: Amur maackia is tolerant of all but the worst soils.

Robinia × ambigua 'Idahoensis'

(ro-BI-nee-a am-BIG-wa) **Idaho locust,** will grow in all climates, LSP, ESU. ○ ◐ 🐝
Size: 30 to 40 feet tall, 15 to 30 feet wide
Flower Color: Rose
Water: Best with occasional deep waterings.
Characteristics: An open, airy, deciduous tree of hybrid origin, Idaho locust has a graceful, fine-textured appeal. Mid-green, foot-long compound leaves are made up of more than a dozen small, rounded leaflets. This fast-growing tree does not self-sow like its troublesome parent, the black locust. The showy, deep pink flowers are fragrant and borne in drooping, 8-inch clusters like those of wisteria, sometimes attracting hummingbirds. Idaho locust tolerates strong wind. It is susceptible to Texas root rot in hot climates. The cultivar 'Idahoensis Purple Robe' has even darker flowers over a longer period, with reddish new growth.
Cultural Information: Can tolerate any soil. Do not prune in spring, for it bleeds.

ADDITIONAL WATERWISE TREES FOR COLD, DRY CLIMATES

Celtis occidentalis hackberry ◐
Corylus colurna Turkish filbert
Elaeagnus angustifolia Russian olive W 🐝
Gymnocladus dioica Kentucky coffee tree
Juniperus juniper tree 🐝
Koelreuteria paniculata goldenrain tree ◐

Pinus aristata bristlecone pine
Pinus edulis pinyon pine
Pinus ponderosa ponderosa pine
Ptelea trifoliata wafer ash, hop tree ◐
Quercus gambelii Gambel oak, encino
Quercus macrocarpa bur oak

Waterwise Shrubs for Cold, Dry Climates

Cercocarpus ledifolius

(sur-ko-KAR-pus le-di-FO-lee-us) **curl-leaf mountain mahogany, palo duro,** Native American, also good in hot, dry climates. ○
Size: 6 to 12 feet tall and wide
Flower Color: Insignificant
Water: Little to none once established.
Characteristics: Curl-leaf mountain mahogany is an open-branching shrub with narrow, lance-shaped, 1-inch dark-green leaves. These leathery, thick leaves curl under along the margins and are white beneath. Curl-leaf mountain mahogany is the only broad-leaf evergreen shrub that is hardy and drought-tolerant in cold, dry climates. Its fruits have feathery 1- to 2-inch plumes that catch the sunlight and persist into winter. The wood is very hard, hence the English and Spanish common names. It is native over a broad range of the mountainous West, thriving in poor, rocky soil and on slopes. Curl-leaf mountain mahogany is excellent for erosion control. Closely related is the smaller, more fine-textured little-leaf mountain mahogany, *C. intricatus*, with very silvery branches and twigs and about 4 feet tall and wide. It is not quite as

hardy. *C. montanus* is of lesser garden value as it is not evergreen.

Cultural Information: Needs a well-drained soil.

Fallugia paradoxa (fa-LOO-ji-a pa-ra-DO-xa) **Apache plume,** Native American, also does well in hot, dry climates, LSP, SU, F. ○ ❀

Size: 3 to 6 feet tall and wide

Flower Color: White

Water: None, once established.

Characteristics: A fine-textured deciduous to semievergreen, multibranched shrub, Apache plume is native to dry rocky soil throughout much of the Southwest, yet is very cold-hardy. Dainty dark green, many-lobed leaves, tawny or silver beneath, turn rusty and persist in warmer regions. The slender stems are silver; older bark is shredding. Showy white, 1-inch flowers are produced heavily in late spring, then on and off well into autumn. They resemble single wild roses and are visited by butterflies. The early crop quickly matures to wonderful rosy peach, fluffy fruit, with feathery tails like rosy smoke over the plant, unforgettable when backlit by the sun. These fruits persist as more flowers bloom, creating a lovely effect. Apache plume is useful to control erosion.

Cultural Information: Any well-drained soil will do.

Rosa (RO-sa) **hardy shrub roses,** Europe, Asia, North America, will grow in most climates except the hottest and most humid, SP, ESU, SU. ○ ◑ ❀

Size: Varies with species

Flower Colors: White, pink, rose, yellow, orange

Water: Occasional deep watering is best.

Characteristics: There are several hardy, drought-tolerant shrub roses that need none of the pampering—water, fertilizer, winter protection, pruning and pest control—that the modern hybrids do. All are deciduous and have compound leaves made up of oval leaflets on arching, sparsely branched, thorny stems. Many bear showy orange or red fruits called hips. Except for rugosa and Woods rose, they bloom only once for a period of several weeks in spring or early summer. *Rosa × harisonii,* Harison's yellow rose, is a famous pioneer rose also known as the yellow rose of Texas. It survives on abandoned homesteads all across the West. It grows 6 to 8 inches tall and wide, forming a dense, suckering, thorny mass. The 2- to 3-inch, semidouble flowers are fragrant and a rich deep yellow, blooming in late spring and early summer. *R. foetida,* the Austrian briar, is best known in its two smaller, showier forms, *R. f. bicolor,* the Austrian copper rose, and *R. f. persiana,* the Persian yellow rose. Both of these bloom in spring and grow 5 feet tall and 4 feet wide, into an open, vase-shaped, prickly bush. Austrian copper has single, brilliant orange, 2-inch flowers; Persian yellow's flowers are fully double, cupped bright yellow affairs. Plants look best when old wood is pruned out. *R. glauca* (*R. rubrifolia*), the redleaf rose,

Fallugia paradoxa

Rosa rugosa 'Jens Munk'

hips of Rosa glauca

is grown primarily for its great foliage and fruits. A gangly 5- to 8-foot-tall shrub, it sends up arching maroon-purple canes clothed in silvery plum-copper foliage. In light, dry shade, this rose is more silver than maroon. Small, 1-inch, single pink flowers in early summer become drooping orange, cherrylike hips. *R. rugosa* ❀ grows 3 to 6 feet tall and often twice as wide. It is a remarkably tough, yet lush, thickly leaved, thorny shrub rose. The foliage is dark green, pleated, leathery and slightly glossy. Large, 3- to 4-inch fragrant, single or semidouble flowers bloom on and off all summer. Showy, 1-inch orange-red hips make a tart jelly. Sometimes the plants exhibit good yellow and burgundy fall color. Rugosa roses make an impenetrable hedge and are excellent for erosion control. They take strong wind and seaside conditions. A few of the better cultivars are: 'Blanc Double de Coubert', 2 to 3 feet tall and 4 to 5 feet wide with white semidouble flowers; 'Fru Dagmar Hastrup', similar compact size, with soft pink single flowers; 'Alba', 6 feet tall and wide with white single flowers and excellent fruit; 'Agnes', also large, with double butterscotch-buff flowers; 'Martin Frobisher', 4 feet tall and wide with double soft pink flowers; 'Scabrosa', large, with single deep rose flowers and excellent fruit; 'Jens Munk', 4 feet tall and wide, with clear pink double flowers; and 'Schneezwerg', also known as 'Snowdwarf', only 2 feet tall, with white semidouble flowers and good fruit. *R. woodsii,* ❀ Woods rose, is native to the Rocky Mountain region. It is a large, suckering shrub, to 9 feet tall and often wider, with pink single, 1- to 2-inch flowers that bloom on and off for two months. The foliage is fine-textured yet lush, a soft, almost opalescent blue-green. Small, profuse cherrylike hips persist all winter, attractive against the maroon and purple canes. Woods rose tolerates part shade. Refer to plant portraits for cold, humid climates for other suitable rose species.

Cultural Information: Prune old, dried canes to the ground during the dormant season every few years for appearance and to promote new growth. These roses will grow in all but the very worst soils. Good air circulation is helpful to ward off potential pests and diseases.

Syringa vulgaris

Syringa (si-RIN-ga) **lilac,** Asia, Southern Europe, will grow in most climates. For areas with hot summers and mild winters, cut-leaf, Persian, Chinese and the Descanso hybrids of the common lilac are best, SP, ESU. ○ ◐ 🐞

Size: Varies with species

Flower Colors: Lilac, purple, rose, pink, white

Water: Occasional deep watering is helpful, especially around and just after flowering.

Characteristics: Lilacs are deciduous shrubs with showy panicles of flowers, often highly fragrant. These are frequented by butterflies and hummingbirds in warmer climates. *S. laciniata,* cut-leaf lilac, has the best foliage of the group—finely cut and deep green. It grows 6 to 8 feet tall, with flowers that are small, dainty and pale lavender. *S. meyeri,* Meyer lilac, is a rounded, dense shrub 4 to 8 feet tall and 6 to 10 feet wide. It is the most floriferous lilac, covering itself with 4-inch violet panicles in late spring. Meyer lilac tolerates light dry shade and doesn't suffer from the mildew that plagues the common lilac. 'Palibin' is a compact 4-foot cultivar. *S. microphylla,* the littleleaf lilac, has small, 1-inch rounded leaves that give it a delicate appearance. It is a dense, twiggy, wide-spreading, rounded shrub, 4 to 6 feet tall and 6 to 10 feet wide. The flowers are small and dainty, a lavender-rose color, appearing several weeks later than Meyer and the common lilac. They are fragrant and will bloom here and there through the summer and into fall. 'Superba' is a nice form with many deep pink flowers. *S. patula* 'Miss Kim', Korean or Manchurian lilac, is a compact, upright 4- to 6-foot shrub. Its foliage is similar to that of the common lilac, but a darker, richer green and not as prone to mildew. Large, pale

lavender, fragrant panicles bloom a bit later than the common lilac. *S. × persica* is a graceful, open shrub 4 to 8 feet tall and wide, with many fragrant, 3-inch lilac flower clusters. The 2-inch foliage is narrow. *S. villosa*, *S. reflexa* and *S. × prestoniae* are all coarser, later-blooming shrubs, 6 to 10 feet tall and wide, grown particularly for their remarkable hardiness. They bloom profusely on stout, upright stems. The flowers have little fragrance. 'James MacFarlane' is a well-known pink-flowered cultivar. *S. × hyacinthiflora* and *S. oblata* are similarly bone-hardy, large and coarse, yet bloom earlier than all the other lilacs and have good maroon fall color. *S. vulgaris*, common lilac, is a coarse, upright, suckering shrub generally 8 to 10 feet tall and wide, that can reach up to 20 feet in height. Its large, heart-shaped leaves are prone to mildew in late summer and fall, which is ugly but will not harm the plant much. The large, 6- to 8-inch flower panicles are what made this shrub so well-known and loved. There are too many hybrids to mention. A few of the best and most available are: 'Hugo Koster', single red-purple; 'President Lincoln', single almost-blue; 'Andenken an Ludwig Spaeth', double wine-red; 'Madame Lemoine', double white; 'President Grévy', double lilac-blue.
Cultural Information: Remove a few of the oldest wood to the ground every couple of years after flowering to rejuvenate lilacs. Well-drained, slightly alkaline soil is preferred.

ADDITIONAL WATER-WISE SHRUBS FOR COLD, DRY CLIMATES

Amorpha leadplant

Arctostaphylos manzanita ◐

Artemisia sagebrush 🐢

Atriplex saltbush, chamiso

Caragana pea shrub 🐢

Ceratoides (Eurotia) lanata winterfat

Chamaebatiaria millefolium fernbush 🐢

Chrysothamnus rabbitbrush, chamisa

Cytisus broom (some hardy forms) W 🐢

Cowania mexicana cliff rose 🐢

Ephedra joint fir

Fendlera rupicola cliff fendler bush 🐢

Forestiera neomexicana New Mexico privet

Holodiscus dumosus rock spirea ◐

Hypericum kalmianum St. John's wort ◐

Juniperus juniper 🐢

Lonicera shrub honeysuckle ◐ W 🐢

Peraphyllum ramosissimum squaw apple

Philadelphus mock orange ◐ 🐢

Prunus besseyi sand cherry

Purshia tridentata bitterbrush, antelope bush 🐢

Rhamnus smithii Smith buckthorn

Rhus sumac ◐ (see shrub portrait, page 66) 🐢

Ribes currant 🐢 ◐

Rubus deliciosus boulder raspberry ◐

Shepherdia buffaloberry

Symphoricarpos snowberry, coralberry ◐

Lathyrus latifolius
'Albus'

Waterwise Vine for Cold, Dry Climates

Lathyrus latifolius (LA-thi-rus la-ti-FO-lee-us) **perennial pea vine,** Europe, will grow in any climate, ESU, SU, F. ○ ◐ ✿

Size: Up to 10 feet
Flower Colors: Rose, pink, white
Water: None necessary.
Characteristics: Perennial pea vine is a tough, old-fashioned vine long grown and naturalized in the United States but rarely available for sale. It has gray-green foliage and winged stems, and clasps onto other plants or any other thin support by tendrils. Showy 1-inch flowers appear in 6-inch clusters over a long period in summer. They are not fragrant. Perennial pea vine makes a good cut flower. It self-sows. Cultivars 'Albus' and 'White Pearl' are white-flowered; 'Splendens' has bicolored, deep rose and purple flowers. *L. grandiflorus* is similar, with smaller flower clusters and leaves, not as robust nor as

hardy. *L. rotundifolius* is the daintiest of the perennial pea vines, with small, sparse, rounded leaflets, thin stems and bicolored rose and purple flowers. It is not quite as hardy. *Cultural Information:* Perennial pea vines grow in any soil. Remove spent flower clusters to keep them in flower longer—they will bloom for four months if kept deadheaded.

COLD, HUMID CLIMATES

Amelanchier *sp.*

Waterwise Trees for Cold, Humid Climates

Amelanchier hybrids (a-me-LAN-keer) **serviceberry, shadblow,** Native American, grows in most climates except the very hottest, ESP. ○ ◑
Size: 20 to 30 feet tall, 10 to 15 feet wide
Flower Colors: White, blush pink
Water: Occasional deep watering is desirable.
Characteristics: There are many serviceberries native to North America; all are attractive, deciduous small trees or large shrubs. Their early flowers, appearing before the leaves unfurl, gave rise to the common name, for in the North, settlers' early spring burial services when the ground thawed coincided with the tree's bloom. Hybrid serviceberries have showier, larger, more profuse flowers than the species and better drought tolerance. The 1-inch, five-petaled flowers are reminiscent of apple blossoms. Red fruits develop by early summer, turning dark blue and quickly eaten by birds. The broadly oval, 2- to 3-inch foliage is reddish upon emerging, turning green and then a rich orange-red in the fall. Hybrid serviceberries also have nice, smooth, light gray bark. *A.* × 'Cumulus' has an upright habit, making it a good single-trunked tree. It produces a froth of white flowers. *A.* × *grandiflora* 'Robin Hill' and 'Rubescens' have rosy buds that open to blush pink flowers. *Cultural Information:* Serviceberries are tolerant of most soils. A cooling mulch is helpful.

Sorbus alnifolia (SOR-bus al-ni-FO-lee-a) **Korean mountain ash,** Asia, can also grow well in cold, dry climates if given extra water, LSP, ESU. ○
Size: 40 to 60 feet tall, almost as wide
Flower Color: White
Water: Occasional deep watering is helpful.
Characteristics: This deciduous, rounded tree has foliage not commonly seen in a mountain ash; it is elm- or beechlike rather than the typical pinnate leaves. Leaves are oval and a rich dark green, turning amber and orange in the fall. Korean mountain ash also has lovely, beechlike, smooth gray bark. ¾-inch flowers are in showy, white flat-topped clusters, turning into wonderful crimson berries that persist all autumn (until the birds get desperate). This tree tolerates high winds. The cultivar 'Redbird' has a more upright, narrow form.
Cultural Information: This is the least pest-ridden and most drought-tolerant of the mountain ashes. Does well in almost any soil of moderate fertility.

Syringa reticulata (si-RIN-ga re-ti-kew-LA-ta) **Japanese tree lilac,** Japan, does well in cold, dry climates and the cooler parts of mild maritime climates, ESU, SU. ○ ◑
Size: 30 feet tall and almost as wide
Flower Color: Creamy white
Water: Occasional deep watering is preferable.
Characteristics: Japanese tree lilac is a deciduous, rounded tree. The somewhat coarse-textured oval leaves are 3 to 6 inches long. Foot-long, showy panicles of creamy flowers bloom for a few weeks in early to midsummer; their fragrance is not particularly good, but not awful, either. Reddish-brown, shiny bark looks like that of a cherry's until very old, when it

Sorbus alnifolia

turns rougher and more gray. Cultivars: 'Ivory Silk' is a smaller, more compact plant; 'Summer Snow' is especially floriferous.

Cultural Information: Any moderately fertile, well-drained soil will do.

Ulmus parvifolia (UL-mus par-vi-FO-lee-a) **lacebark elm,** China, will grow in all but the very coldest and hottest climates. ○ ◑

Size: 30 to 60 feet tall, 50 to 70 feet wide

Flower Color: Insignificant

Water: Best with occasional deep watering

Characteristics: This graceful, fast-growing yet strong-wooded tree is somewhat fine-textured and has a broad crown. Small 1- to 2-inch, dark green, glossy leaves stay on late into the fall, sometimes turning yellow or burgundy before dropping. In the mildest climates, above 25° F., lacebark elm is evergreen. It has lovely bark with buff, orange and gray mottling similar to that of the sycamore. It is resistant to oak root fungus, but susceptible to Texas root rot in very hot climates. The cultivars 'Drake', 'Sempervirens' and 'Pendens' have a more weeping form, while 'Emerald Vase' is large, upright and vase-shaped, similar to the blighted American elm. 'True Green' is the best for evergreen character in mild climates. 'Ohio' has all the best qualities of the species. Lacebark elm is sometimes called Chinese elm, as is the much inferior Siberian elm, *Ulmus pumila*, which is weak-wooded, disease- and pest-rid-den and weedy. Do not confuse these trees.

Cultural Information: Lacebark elm is a highly disease- and insect-free elm. It does best in a deep, well-drained soil but can tolerate almost any sort.

ADDITIONAL WATERWISE TREES FOR COLD, HUMID CLIMATES

Acanthopanax sieboldianus five-leaf aralia ◑

Acer campestre hedge maple

Acer ginnala Amur maple

Acer tataricum Tatarian maple

Ailanthus altissima tree of heaven ◑ W

Aralia elata angelica tree ◑

Carpinus betulus European hornbeam

Carya hickory

Catalpa speciosa catalpa (see tree portrait, page 59) 🐢

Celtis occidentalis hackberry ◑

Cercis redbud ◑ (see tree portraits, pages 55 and 70)

Cladrastis yellowwood 🐢

Corylus colurna Turkish filbert

Crataegus hawthorn (see tree portrait, page 59)

Diospyros virginiana persimmon

Eucommia ulmoides hardy rubber tree, gutta-percha tree

Euonymus europaea spindle tree

Fraxinus pennsylvanica green ash—improved cultivars

Ginkgo biloba ginkgo (see tree portrait, page 55)

Gleditsia triacanthos honey locust 🐢

Gymnocladus dioicas Kentucky coffee tree

Juglans nigra black walnut

Juniperus juniper tree 🐢

Syringa reticulata

Koelreuteria paniculata goldenrain tree

Maackia amurensis Amur maackia (see tree portrait, page 60) 🐢

Maclura pomifera osage orange W

Parrotia persica parrotia

Phellodendron cork tree

Picea omorika Serbian spruce

Picea pungens Colorado spruce

Pinus many are waterwise

Prunus americana American plum 🐢

Prunus maackii Amur chokecherry 🐢

Ptelea trifoliata wafer ash, hop tree ◑

Quercus many oaks are waterwise in this region

Robinia × ambigua 'Idahoensis' Idaho locust (see tree portrait, page 60) 🐢

Robinia pseudoacacia black locust W 🐢

Tamarix salt cedar, tamarisk

Tilia linden 🐢

Viburnum prunifolium blackhaw

Xanthoceras sorbifolium yellowhorn

Ulmus parvifolia

Waterwise Shrubs for Cold, Humid Climates

Myrica pensylvanica

(MI-ri-ka pen-sil-VA-ni-ka) **northern bayberry,** Native American, grows in other climates if not too hot. ○ ◑ 🦋

Size: 5 to 10 feet tall and wide
Flower Color: Inconspicuous
Water: Best with occasional deep watering.

Characteristics: Northern bayberry is a dense, upright shrub, usually deciduous, although the leaves hang on late into fall. The wonderfully aromatic foliage is narrow, leathery and somewhat glossy, and an attractive, rich green. Female plants bear huge quantities of small grayish-white, bloomy berries from inconspicuous early spring flowers. The berries are most ornamental in late fall, winter and early spring when the foliage is absent. Northern bayberry is native all along the Eastern seaboard and thrives in seaside conditions, strong winds and infertile soils. Fragrant bayberry candles are made from the waxy fruit. Bayberry is an excellent plant for erosion control and resists oak root fungus. If happy in its site, it may sucker and form a colony. 'Wildwood' is an especially attractive selection.

Cultural Information: Northern bayberry prefers a sandy, well-drained, infertile, acidic soil, but will grow in any if not too alkaline. It responds to harsh pruning; you can cut one-third to the ground every year to rejuvenate the shrub. Plant both male and female plants for the most berries.

Myrica pensylvanica

Potentilla fruticosa

(po-ten-TI-la froo-ti-KO-sa) **shrubby potentilla,** widespread across Northern hemisphere, grows in other climates if not exceedingly hot, F. ○ ◑ ✿ ❅

Size: 2 to 5 feet tall and wide
Flower Colors: Yellow, white, peach, orange, blush pink
Water: Best with occasional deep watering.

Characteristics: Shrubby potentillas are long-flowering, fine-textured, small deciduous shrubs. 1- to 2-inch flowers, looking like small single roses, stud the bushy mounds. Small, divided foliage varies from deep green to gray-green, and is deer resistant. Too many cultivars exist to list all here; some of the better are: 'Abbotswood', 2 to 3 feet, white flowers on dark green foliage; 'Coronation Triumph', 3 to 4 feet, with abundant bright yellow flowers; 'Daydawn', 3 feet with peach-flushed white flowers, best in part shade; 'Goldfinger', 2 feet with very large golden flowers; 'Katherine Dykes', 2 to 3 feet, many pale yellow flowers; 'Primrose Beauty', 3 feet with large, soft yellow flowers and gray-green foliage; 'Sophie's Blush', 2 feet, blush pink, best in part shade; 'Tangerine', 2 to 3 feet, yellow suffused with orange, best in part shade; 'Vilmoriniana', 5 feet, silvery leaves, creamy pale yellow flowers.

Cultural Information: Prune out weak, twiggy growth and dead wood. Shrubby potentillas tolerate any adequately drained soil, clay included, preferring slightly alkaline conditions.

Rhus (roos) **sumac,** Native

American, does well in all but the hottest climates, where *R. ovata,* sugarbush and *R. virens,* both evergreen, are best, ESU, SU. ○

Size: Dependent on species
Flower Colors: Greenish, yellow, not very showy
Water: Little to none once established.

Characteristics: Sumacs are grown for their lovely foliage, showy fruits and great orange, red or burgundy fall color. They tend to sucker and grow into colonies, so need adequate space in the garden. They will often self-sow. They are good for erosion control, and where

Potentilla fruticosa
'Katherine Dykes'

necessary, serve well as fire-retardant plantings. Birds like the fruits. *R. aromatica*, fragrant sumac, is a 4- to 6-foot tall, wide-spreading deciduous shrub native to the eastern half of the United States. Small clusters of yellow flowers appear in spring, followed by clusters of bright orange-red fruits in summer. The three-lobed leaves are somewhat glossy, rich green and pleasantly aromatic when bruised. Fragrant sumac is resistant to oak root fungus and has good, orange-red fall color. It can be sheared into a hedge. Cultivars to look for are 'Gro-low', 2 feet tall and 6 feet wide; 'Green Mound', 4 feet tall and 6 feet wide; and 'Green Globe', 6 feet tall and wide. *R. trilobata*, three-leaf sumac, lemita or squaw bush, is native to the western half of the United States and very similar to fragrant sumac, except the leaves are somewhat smaller and more leathery, and their fragrance is acrid. Squaw bush is also a bit more drought-tolerant. *R. copallina*, shining sumac; *R. glabra*, smooth sumac; and *R. typhina*, staghorn sumac, are all large, open, suckering deciduous shrubs 10 to 25 feet tall and wide that can grow into small trees. They have pinnately compound, ferny leaves that turn brilliant orange and scarlet in fall. Their showy, cone-shaped fruit clusters turn red in late summer and remain effective through the winter. Shining sumac has the most beautiful glossy leaves of the lot. Staghorn sumac has hairy new growth, and both it and smooth sumac have cultivars

with finely dissected foliage— 'Laciniata' and 'Dissecta'. These sumacs make great winter silhouettes—dark, gaunt, ascending, gnarly branches with rusty brown fruits at the tips. A smaller variety, *R. glabra* var. *cismontana*, native to the Rockies, grows to only 3 feet with slightly smaller foliage.
Cultural Information: Sumacs grow well in any soil.

Rosa (RO-sa) **hardy shrub roses,** Europe, Asia, North America, will grow in all climates, need more water in hot, dry climates, SP, ESU, SU. ○ 🌻

Size: Varies with species
Flower Colors: Pink, rose, yellow, white
Characteristics: The following shrub roses are tough, cold-hardy and water-wise, unlike their pampered relatives the modern hybrids. They bloom only once, for two to three weeks in spring or summer, unless noted otherwise. These roses are carefree, offering flowers and attractive foliage and fruits. *R. × alba* cultivars have lush, gray-green foliage and wonderfully fragrant flowers in late spring and early summer. Excellent old-fashioned selections include: 'Königin von Dänemark', 5 feet tall and wide, pink double; 'Maiden's Blush', same size, paler blush pink; 'Madame Plantier', to 10 feet with white double flowers; 'Semiplena', 8 feet tall and 5 feet wide, semi-double white flowers in great profusion, excellent orange hips; 'Félicité Parmentier', smaller at 4 feet tall and wide with flat, very double, blush pink flow-

Rhus typhina
'Laciniata'

Rosa 'Frühlingsgold'

ers; and 'Celestial', 6 feet tall and 4 feet wide, with semi-double, soft pink flowers. *R. eglanteria*, the sweet briar rose, is a fine-textured, large, twiggy shrub growing 8 to 12 feet tall and not quite as wide. It is very thorny and bears many small 1-inch, pink, single flowers in late spring, followed by a large crop of small, cherry-red hips. The foliage has a delicious apple scent on warm, humid days and after a rain, hence the common name. It can be sheared into an informal hedge. *R. hugonis*, the Father Hugo rose, is a large, 6- to 8-foot arching, fine-textured shrub

Rosa × alba 'Maiden's Blush'

with dainty, ferny foliage and maroon canes. The arching stems are lined with pale yellow, single, lightly fragrant, 1- to 2-inch flowers in mid-spring, perfect with lilacs. Sometimes it displays a nice amber-orange fall color. *R. setigera*, the prairie rose, is a large arching rose native to the Midwest. It grows 5 feet tall and much wider, up to 15 feet in girth if allowed to sprawl and trail to its heart's content. Single, 2-inch, deep pink, barely fragrant flowers appear in midsummer, fading to blush, followed by small, rounded red hips. The somewhat glossy, deep green foliage often takes on warm fall tones of crimson, purple, orange and yellow. The stems are reddish when young. *R. spinosissima*, the Scotch or burnet rose, gave rise to several excellent, highly fragrant, tough shrub roses. 'Altaica' grows to 6 feet, with gray-green foliage and large, 3-inch single, white flowers in late spring that turn to plum-colored hips in the fall. 'Stanwell Perpetual' is similar but smaller, and its loosely double flowers have a blush of pink and bloom on and off into the fall. 'Frühlingsgold' bears a heavy crop of butter yellow, almost single, 3-inch flowers on a 6-foot-tall, vigorous bush; 'Frühlingsmorgen' has single, rose pink flowers with cream and yellow centers on a similar shrub. These all tolerate seacoast conditions and poor soil. *R. virginiana*, the Virginia rose, is native to the East Coast. It grows to 6 feet tall and wide, an upright, dense bush with lush, dark green foliage that takes on rich autum-

nal tints of orange, red and amber. Clear pink, fragrant, 2-inch, single flowers bloom in midsummer, turning to orange-red rounded hips that persist well into winter—especially attractive against the reddish canes. Virginia rose tolerates seaside conditions and any soil, even sandy, infertile ones. Other tough, water-wise shrub roses good for cold, humid climates are *R. glauca* and *R. rugosa*—refer to their plant portraits for cold, dry climates. Harison's yellow rose and *R. foetida* suffer from black spot in high humidity.

Cultural Information: These tough, carefree roses do well in all but the poorest soils, but respond to soil improvement. Prune a few of the oldest and weakest canes to the base every few years to rejuvenate.

ADDITIONAL WATER-WISE SHRUBS FOR COLD, HUMID CLIMATES

Aronia chokeberry ◖

Berberis koreana Korean barberry 🐢

Berberis thunbergii, cultivars Japanese barberry 🐢

Caragana pea shrub 🐢

Ceanothus americanus New Jersey tea, mountain sweet

Cotinus smokebush (see shrub portrait, page 57)

Cytisus broom (some hardy forms) W 🐢

Deutzia

Hippophae rhamnoides sea buckthorn

Holodiscus dumosus rock spirea

Hypericum kalmianum, H. prolificum St. John's wort ◖

Juniperus juniper 🐢

Kolkwitzia amabilis beauty bush

Ligustrum privet, deciduous spp. ◖ W 🐢

Lonicera shrubby honeysuckle ◖ W 🐢

Microbiota decussata ◖

Philadelphus mock orange 🐢

Physocarpus ninebark

Pinus dwarf forms of pines

Potentilla fruticosa shrubby potentilla (see shrub portrait, page 66)

Prinsepia sinensis cherry prinsepia 🐢

Prunus besseyi sand cherry 🐢

Prunus maritima beach plum 🐢

Prunus tomentosa Nanking cherry 🐢

Rhamnus buckthorn

Rhododendron periclymenoides/ nudiflorum pinxterbloom azalea ◖ 🐢

Rhododendron prinophyllum/roseum roseshell azalea ◖ 🐢

Rhodotypos scandens jet bead ◖

Ribes currant 🐢 ◖

Rubus deliciosus boulder raspberry ◖

Shepherdia buffaloberry

Spiraea spirea

Symphoricarpos snowberry, coralberry ◖

Symplocos paniculata sapphireberry ◖ 🐢

Syringa lilac (see shrub portrait, page 62) 🐢

Viburnum lantana 'Mohican' wayfaring bush

Viburnum × rhytidophylloides hybrid viburnum

Waterwise Vines for Cold, Humid Climates

Lonicera sempervirens
(lo-NI-se-ra sem-per-VI-renz) **trumpet honeysuckle, coral honeysuckle,** Native American, will grow in most other climates, LSP, SU. ○ ◖ ✿

Lonicera sempervirens 'Sulphurea'

Size: 10 to 20 feet
Flower Colors: Red, orange, yellow
Water: Responds to occasional deep watering.
Characteristics: Trumpet honeysuckle is a well-behaved semi-evergreen, twining vine. It has sparse, 2- to 3-inch, blue-green, rounded leaves in pairs along its sinuous stems. The leaves may have a purple tint when young. The showy 3-inch flower clusters are red-orange or yellow and bloom for many weeks; they are frequented by hummingbirds. Pretty red berries follow for two months in the fall—if the birds aren't too hungry. In warmer climates this vine is evergreen and begins blooming in mid-spring. Trumpet honeysuckle tolerates wind, cold and heat. Named cultivars are available for flower color: red, 'Magnifica'; orange, 'Su-perba'; and yellow, 'Sulphurea'.
Cultural Information: Most soils satisfy this vine. Do not prune severely, for it is a slow grower.

ADDITIONAL WATERWISE VINES FOR COLD, HUMID CLIMATES

Campsis radicans trumpet creeper
Lathyrus latifolius perennial pea vine

MILD, MARITIME CLIMATES

Waterwise Trees for Mild, Maritime Climates

Acacia (a-KAY-shuh) **acacia, wattle,** some Native American, some Australian, will also grow in hot, dry climates, W, ESP, SP. ○ ❀
Size: Varies with species
Flower Colors: Yellow, white (rarely)
Water: Little to none necessary once established.
Characteristics: Acacias are easy-to-please, fast-growing trees and large shrubs. They flower in great abundance, in fluffy spikes or puff balls. The flowers are often fragrant, attracting hummingbirds and bees, from which good honey can be made. Leaves vary by species; some are evergreen, some deciduous. Many species have lacy compound leaves; some have phyllodes, flattened leaf stalks, in place of leaves. Acacias tend to grow quickly, and some are short-lived, only 20 to 30 years. Some have thorns. The fruit is a pod; both falling fruit and deciduous leaves can be a problem if neatness is desired. The pollen of Australian species tends to be more allergenic than that of native American species. Many acacias tolerate heat and wind, and make good seashore plants. There are hundreds of acacia species, including a number of good shrubs and groundcovers useful for hillsides and erosion control. *A. baileyana,* known as cootamundra wattle and Bailey's mimosa, is a graceful evergreen, Australian species that grows 20 to 40 feet tall. It has beautiful feathery, blue-gray leaves and fragrant yellow flowers in clusters in late winter. It lacks thorns. The cultivar 'Purpurea' has new growth tinted purple. *A. greggii* is native to the Southwest. Its common name, catclaw acacia, refers to its curved thorns. A large deciduous shrub or small tree growing 10 to 20 feet tall with a similar spread, it has fine-textured, gray-green foliage. Fragrant, pale yellow to creamy white flowers appear in late spring and may rebloom later. It is hardier than *A. baileyana,* to 0° F. *A. minuta/A. smallii* is another southwestern native, called huisache or sweet acacia for its fragrant yellow puffball flowers in spring. It is a thorny, small tree, 20 to 35 feet tall and 15 to 25 feet wide, with feathery, deciduous leaves. It withstands colder temperatures than cootamundra wattle, to 10° F. *A. podalyriifolia,* pearl acacia, grows 10 to 20 feet tall and 12 to 15 feet wide, and must be pruned to become a tree. Small, rounded phyllodes give this tree a soft, silvery-gray cast. Long, pale yellow flower clusters appear in winter. *A. saligna/A. cyanophylla,* known as blue-leaf wattle for its narrow,

Acacia schaffneri

Cercis occidentalis

evergreen, blue-tinted foliage, grows to 20 to 30 feet tall and 15 to 20 feet wide. This multi-stemmed Australian tree blooms in early spring with masses of deep golden balls. It is hardy to 20° F. *A. schaffneri* is called twisted acacia for its interesting form. A deciduous small tree up to 20 feet tall and wide, it sports finely divided, semievergreen foliage and fragrant yellow balls in spring. This Mexican native needs some pruning to show off its lovely shape; be careful of small thorns hidden in its leaves. Hardy to 20° F.

Cultural Information: Acacias tolerate most soils, but good drainage is a must. Most species tend to grow multi-stemmed, so if a single-trunked tree is desired, remove lower branches and all but the best stem at a young age and stake until strong. Some species sprout on their trunk and at the base, so a bit of regular pruning is advised for best appearance. Acacias are easy to grow from seed, so you can experiment with less available species—nick the hard seed coat with a file before sowing.

Maytenus boaria

Cercis occidentalis (SUR-sis o-xi-den-TA-lis) **western red-bud,** Native American, will grow in other climates except those with severely cold winters, see related species for better-adapted choices for those climates, LW, SP. ○ ◑
Size: 10 to 18 feet tall and wide
Flower Color: Rich rose-pink
Water: Little necessary once established.
Characteristics: Western redbud is cousin to the larger eastern and Mexican redbuds. Native to dry foothill slopes in California, it tolerates more sun and a drier site than the others. It grows slowly into a small, multi-stemmed tree. Western redbud has year-'round appeal: Just as the growing season begins, its bare branches are smothered in clusters of small, brilliant rose, pea-shaped flowers for two to three weeks. After the flowers finish, the deciduous foliage unfurls into attractive heart-shaped, blue-green leaves. In autumn the foliage turns a warm yellow, and in cooler climates or higher elevations sometimes a crimson red. In winter the bare, reddish-brown twigs and bark and persistent seed pods make an attractive silhouette. It is a good tree for hillsides and erosion control. The best bloom occurs in areas with some frost. This small tree resists oak root fungus.
Cultural Information: Western redbud needs a fast-draining soil, the looser and coarser the better.

Maytenus boaria (may-TEN-us bo-AR-ee-a) **mayten tree,** Chile, will grow in hot, dry climates as well. ○ ◑
Size: 30 to 50 feet tall, 20 feet wide

Flower Color: Insignificant
Water: Occasional deep waterings once established.
Characteristics: Mayten tree is a broadly spreading, yet airy, evergreen tree. Its branches hang gracefully much like those of the weeping willow. Rich green, 1- to 2-inch, narrow leaves add to the willowlike effect. It can be grown as a multistemmed or single-trunk specimen. It grows somewhat slowly. 'Green Showers' is a good cultivar for dependably attractive form. Mayten tree resists oak root fungus and does well on the seacoast.
Cultural Information: Mayten tree tolerates heat and cold to 15° F. A well-drained, relatively fertile soil is preferable. Avoid frequent shallow waterings and root disturbance or root suckers may be a problem. The shape of this tree varies a great deal among seedlings—judicious pruning of side growth may be necessary.

Melaleuca (me-la-LOO-ka) **paperbark, bottlebrush,** Australia, some species will also grow in hot, dry climates and hot, humid climates, SP, SU, F. ○ ◑ ✿
Size: Varies with species
Flower Colors: Pink, lavender, red, white, cream, yellow
Water: Little, if any, supplemental, once established.
Characteristics: Melaleuca is an evergreen tree and large shrubs related to the showy bottlebrush genus *Callistemon.* Most species are fast-growing and hardy to around 25° F. They are blessed with ornamental bark and foliage, and lovely, long-flowering blossoms.

Prominent stamens give these their bottlebrush appearance and attract hummingbirds. Persistent woody seed capsules can be attractive as well. *M. decussata*, lilac melaleuca, is a small tree that grows 8 to 20 feet tall and wide. Small blue-green leaves give it a fine texture. Its shredding bark is brown; its branches arch gracefully. Lilac, 1-inch flower spikes appear from late spring into summer. Prune, shape and thin to display the attractive bark of the trunks. *M. ericifolia* is called heath melaleuca because its deep green, needle-like leaves resemble those of heather. It reaches 10 to 25 feet. It has fibrous tan or gray bark and creamy, 1-inch flower spikes in spring. Heath melaleuca is especially tolerant of difficult conditions. *M. linariifolia*, flaxleaf paperbark, is not well-suited to windy seacoast conditions. It is a broad spreading, umbrella-shaped tree, 15 to 30 feet tall. The fabulous white bark shreds like paper, similar to paperbark birch in colder climates, hence its common name. It is clothed in stiff, blue-green, needlelike, 1-inch-long leaves and an abundance of snowy white, 2-inch flower spikes in late spring and early summer. *M. nesophylla*, pink melaleuca, grows into a 30-foot-tall, picturesque tree with great character. Gray-green, round, 1-inch leaves and a continual display of 1-inch, mauve flower spikes that fade to white with yellow tips give this adaptable tree year-'round appeal. *M. quinquenervia/leucadendron*, cajeput tree, is known as punk tree in the Deep South,

a wetter climate in which this tree has become a self-seeding weed. An upright single or multistemmed tree 20 to 40 feet tall, it nevertheless has a soft effect in the landscape for its weeping branches. The leaves are narrow, about 3 inches long, covered in silvery hairs when young, then turning green and finally purple-tinted when the weather turns cold. Creamy white, occasionally pink or purple 2- to 3-inch flower spikes appear in late summer and fall. The spongy cream and tan bark strips off. Cajeput tree takes the gamut of difficult conditions. *M. styphelioides* is called prickly melaleuca for its slightly sharp, light green foliage. A 20- to 40-foot-tall tree with weeping branches and an airy appearance, this species offers 1- to 2-inch spikes of creamy white flowers in summer and fall. The papery bark is light tan in color. Prickly melaleuca tolerates heavy soil, seacoast conditions, and is resistant to oak root fungus.

Cultural Information: Most melaleucas are tolerant of any soil except the very alkaline, can take heat and wind, and are well-adapted to seacoast conditions except where noted. They tend to grow multiple trunks; if a single trunk is desired, staking will help the first year. Melaleucas take well to pruning and can even be sheared into hedges.

ADDITIONAL WATERWISE TREES FOR MILD, MARITIME CLIMATES

Aesculus californica California buckeye 🐢

Albizia julibrissin hardy silk tree W 🐢

Arbutus menziesii madrone 🐢

Arbutus unedo strawberry tree 🐢 ◑

Brachychiton populneus bottle tree

Calocedrus decurrens incense cedar 🐢

Casuarina beefwood, she oak

Cedrus cedar

Celtis hackberry ◑

Ceratonia siliqua carob tree (see tree portrait, page 51) 🐢

Chilopsis linearis desert willow 🐢

× *Cupressocyparis leylandii* Leyland cypress

Cupressus cypress (see tree portrait, page 52)

Diospyros kaki oriental persimmon

Eucalyptus gum W 🐢

Ficus carica fruiting fig

Koelreuteria goldenrain tree

Melia azedarach chinaberry, Texas umbrella tree W 🐢

Olea europaea 'Swan Hill' olive

Phoenix canariensis Canary Island date palm

Pinus many

Pistacia pistache (see tree portrait, page 56)

Ptelea trifoliata wafer ash, hop tree ◑

Quercus several native evergreen oaks

Rhus lancea African sumac

Robinia × *ambigua* 'Idahoensis' Idaho locust (see tree portrait, page 60) 🐢

Sapindus soapberry

Schinus molle California pepper tree W 🐢

Sophora japonica Japanese pagoda tree, scholar tree 🐢

Trachycarpus fortunei windmill palm

Ulmus parvifolia lacebark elm (see tree portrait, page 65)

Vitex agnus-castus chaste tree, monk's pepper tree (see tree portrait, page 56) 🐢

Melaleuca styphelioides

Waterwise Shrubs for Mild, Maritime Climates

Bupleurum fruticosum

(bu-PLOO-rum froo-ti-KO-sum) **shrubby bupleurum,** Mediterranean, will grow in all mild-winter climates, LSU. ○ ◑
Size: 5 to 8 feet tall and wide
Flower Color: Yellow
Water: Little, if any, supplemental once established.
Characteristics: Shrubby bupleurum is a large, dense, rounded evergreen shrub. Its narrowly oval, blue-green leaves are 2 to 3 inches long, leathery and glossy. It blooms from mid- to late summer, covered in 3- to 4-inch umbels of green-tinted, yellow flowers.
Cultural Information: This shrub needs good drainage. It is hardy to 5° F. and can survive even lower temperatures but dies down to the ground, acting as a herbaceous perennial. You can shear and prune shrubby bupleurum with impunity. It tolerates seashore conditions well. It is not particularly well-known but can be grown easily from fresh seed that is given a period

Bupleurum fruticosum

Cistus × purpureus

of cold temperatures and moisture.

Cistus

(SIS-tus) **rockrose,** Mediterranean, will grow in other mild-winter climates if nights are cool, SP, ESU. ○ ✿
Size: Varies with species
Flower Colors: White, pink, purple
Water: Little once established.
Characteristics: Rockroses are native to rocky cliffs and are effective planted on hillsides against erosion. Their large, rounded, five-petaled flowers resemble single-flowered roses. Each blossom lasts only one day, dropping its petals by mid-afternoon, but a succession of flowers keeps the plants in bloom for many weeks. Most rockroses have a bushy, mounded, wide-spreading habit. Most are evergreen; leaves are glossy, dark green and leathery, gray and hairy or sticky with fragrant resin, depending on the species. The plants are highly fire-retardant. Rockroses grow quickly and are short-lived if overwatered. They do well in seaside gardens, tolerating wind and salt spray. Deer avoid them. Most are hardy to 15° F. *C. crispus*, 2 to 4 feet tall and twice as wide, has sage green, wavy-edged foliage and long-flowering, 3-inch, orchid pink flowers. *Cistus* × 'Doris Hibberson' is 3 feet tall and wide. It sports gray-green foliage and soft pink, 3-inch flowers. *Cistus* × 'Silver Pink' is shorter at 2 feet, and has narrower, hairier leaves and paler pink flowers. *C. creticus/C. incanus/C. villosus*, known as hairy rockrose, grows 3 to 5 feet tall and wide. It has gray-

felted leaves and purplish-pink, 2-inch flowers. *C. ladanifer*, crimson-spot rockrose, grows into an upright 3- to 5-foot shrub. The large, dark green, sticky, fragrant leaves set off 3-inch white flowers with maroon spots at the base of the petals. *Cistus* × *purpureus*, called orchid rockrose, grows up to 4 feet tall and wide, with gray-green leaves and reddish-purple, 3-inch flowers spotted maroon at base of petals. *C. salviifolius* (incorrectly *C. villosus* 'Prostratus'), known as sageleaf rockrose, is an excellent groundcovering shrub to 2 feet tall, 6 feet or wider. White, 1-inch flowers smother the gray-green crinkled foliage in late spring. It resists verticillium wilt. *C.* × *skanbergii* is a low, broad bush a little over a foot tall and wide, with narrow, gray-green leaves and pale pink, cupped, 1-inch flowers in great profusion in late spring. *C.* × *hybridus/C. corbariensis*, white rockrose, grows 2 to 5 feet tall and much wider. 1½-inch white flowers open from reddish buds over fragrant, crinkled green leaves, which are bronze-tinted in winter. It resists verticillium wilt.
Cultural Information: Rock-roses prefer a neutral to alkaline soil and need good drainage. Loose sandy, rocky or gravelly soils are ideal. Transplant them when young; older plants resent being moved. Do not prune or shear unless absolutely necessary.

Phlomis fruticosa

(FLO-mis froo-ti-KO-sa) **Jerusalem sage,** Mediterranean, grows in other mild-winter climates, ESU, SU. ○

Size: 4 to 6 feet tall and wide
Flower Color: Gold
Water: Will rebloom in summer if given some supplemental watering then.
Characteristics: Jerusalem sage sends up a thicket of vertical stems, much as a perennial does. Showy whorls of lipped golden flowers wrap themselves around the tops of the branches. Large, wrinkled, gray-green foliage, semievergreen and soft and woolly, contrasts nicely with the glowing flowers. New growth is especially woolly and almost white. Jerusalem sage is not attractive to deer and resists oak root fungus.
Cultural Information: Jerusalem sage thrives on poor, rocky, sandy or gravelly soil with excellent drainage. Shear off the top part of stems with spent flowers after blooming to encourage rebloom and improve the bush's appearance.

Trichostema lanatum
(tri-ko-STE-ma la-NA-tum) **woolly blue curls,** Native American, SP, SU. ○ 🐢 ❀
Size: 3 to 6 feet tall and wide
Flower Color: Blue
Water: Little; none during summer.
Characteristics: Woolly blue curls is native to dry California slopes. A fine-textured, rounded, evergreen shrub, it has narrow green foliage similar to rosemary's, with a strong, minty fragrance. Bright blue flowers with showy curled stamens in foot-long woolly spikes (hence the common name) appear for several months in spring and summer, attracting butterflies and hummingbirds. The stems are woolly too. Woolly blue

curls is tolerate of heat and wind.
Cultural Information: Shear spent flower spikes for better appearance and prolonged bloom. Any soil is tolerated as long as drainage is good.

ADDITIONAL WATERWISE SHRUBS FOR MILD, MARITIME CLIMATES

Acacia W 🐢
Alyogyne hugelii blue hibiscus
Arbutus unedo strawberry tree ◐ 🐢
Arctostaphylos manzanita
Buddleya butterfly bush (see shrub portrait, page 57) 🐢
Callicarpa beautyberry
Caryopteris × clandonensis blue mist spirea 🐢
Cassia senna
Ceanothus California lilac 🐢
Cercocarpus mountain mahogany (see shrub portrait, page 60)
Chaenomeles flowering quince
Chamaebatiaria millefolium fern bush 🐢
Comarostaphylis diversifolia summer holly
Convolvulus cneorum bush morning glory
Correa Australian fuchsia 🐢 ◐
Cotinus smokebush (see shrub portrait, page 57)
Cowania mexicana cliff rose 🐢
Cytisus broom W 🐢
Dendromecon bush poppy
Dodonaea viscosa hops bush
Echium fastuosum pride of Madeira
Eriogonum buckwheat (see groundcover portrait, page 82)
Feijoa sellowiana pineapple guava
Fremontodendron flannel bush
Genista broom W 🐢
Grevillea

× *Halimiocistus*
Halimium
Heteromeles arbutifolia toyon ◐
Hypericum St. John's wort ◐
Ilex cornuta Chinese holly
Ilex vomitoria yaupon ◐
Isomeris arborea bladder bush
Juniperus juniper 🐢
Lavandula lavender 🐢
Lavatera tree mallow (see perennial portrait, page 76)
Leptodactylon prickly phlox
Leptospermum tea tree
Ligustrum privet ◐ W 🐢
Lupinus arboreus bush lupine
Nerium oleander oleander 🐢
Prunus ilicifolia holly-leaf cherry ◐ 🐢
Prunus lyonii Catalina cherry 🐢
Punica granatum pomegranate
Raphiolepis Indian hawthorn ◐
Rhamnus buckthorn, coffeeberry ◐
Rhus sumac (see shrub portrait, page 66)
Rosa (species, not hybrids) (see shrub portraits, pages 61, 67) 🐢
Rosmarinus officinalis rosemary
Salvia shrubby sage (see perennial portrait, page 79) 🐢
Santolina lavender cotton 🐢
Senecio (Brachyglottis) daisy bush
Spartium junceum Spanish broom W 🐢
Syringa laciniata (see shrub portrait, page 62) 🐢
Syringa × persica (see shrub portrait, page 63) 🐢
Syringa vulgaris 'Descanso Hybrids' (see shrub portrait, page 63) 🐢
Teucrium fruticans bush germander 🐢
Viburnum tinus laurustinus
Westringia rosmariniformis rosemary westringia

Phlomis fruticosa

Trichostema lanatum

Solanum jasminoides

Waterwise Vines for Mild, Maritime Climates

Solanum jasminoides (so-LA-num jaz-mi-NOY-dees) **potato vine,** Brazil, also grows in hot, humid climates, and hot, dry climates, SP, SU, F. ○ ◑ ❀

Size: 30 feet
Flower Colors: Pale lavender, white
Water: Does best with a deep monthly watering.
Characteristics: Potato vine is a fast-growing, rampant vine that climbs by twining its stems around supports. It is semievergreen, with deep green, oval, 2- to 3-inch leaves that often have a purple cast. These set off the showy flower clusters very well, especially in a partly shaded spot. The plant is rarely out of bloom, but most profuse in spring. Each flower is a 1-inch, five-pointed star with a yellow "beak" of stamens; most clusters are comprised of a dozen blossoms or so. Potato vine is highly fire-retardant, hardy to about 15° to 20° F. and tolerates heat, wind and dry shade. Deer avoid it.
Cultural Information: Potato vine can be cut back hard to encourage vigorous new growth and to clean up a messy old tangle. Takes just about any soil.

ADDITIONAL WATERWISE VINES FOR MILD, MARITIME CLIMATES

Campsis grandiflora Chinese trumpet vine (see vine portrait, page 59)

Lathyrus latifolius perennial pea vine (see vine portrait, page 63)

Lonicera sempervirens trumpet honeysuckle, coral honeysuckle (see vine portrait, page 68)

Macfadyena unguis-cati cat's claw vine, yellow trumpet vine (see vine portrait, page 54)

Wisteria

PERENNIALS

Perennials are perhaps the most adaptable garden plants of all. For this reason, rather than separating them by region as with the woody plants—trees, shrubs and vines—a selection of the very best waterwise perennials follows. Each plant's cultural preferences are clarified, which will help you decide whether the plant is suited to your garden. Some of these plants are shrubby, but because they are either best sheared almost to the ground on an annual basis or because they look more like a herbaceous perennial in size, form and texture, they are included there.

Another great thing about perennials is that they don't require the investment of time and money trees and shrubs do, so I suggest you take some chances and experiment with a wide assortment. Better to count a few losses among the surprising winners than not to have tried at all. What's more, the drier nature of a waterwise garden will help many perennials survive harsher winters than expected, for it is soggy, cold soil as often as cold temperatures in the winter months that does in these plants. Half the perennials thriving in my garden in northern Colorado were supposedly not hardy there, according to books, nursery catalogs and so-called authorities. Consider an unknown perennial an inexpensive, exciting lottery ticket where the odds of winning are actually much, much better than those of a true lottery.

Ten Waterwise Perennials

Asclepias tuberosa (as-KLEE-pee-as tu-be-RO-sa) **butterfly weed,** Native American, grows everywhere, SU. ○ ⬗

Size: 1 to 2 feet
Flower Colors: Orange, yellow, red
Water: Little to none once established; will bloom longer if given occasional deep watering while in flower.
Characteristics: Butterfly weed

Asclepias tuberosa

is one of the showiest North American wildflowers to bloom in midsummer. It grows over a broad range of the eastern half of the continent. Its large, flat-topped clusters of waxy, typically orange, more rarely yellow or red flowers attract many species of butterflies and make good cut flowers. The mid-green, oblong foliage is poisonous to livestock. It looks especially good with deep purple or blue flowers such as those of leadplant, *Amorpha canescens* and is excellent in prairie or meadow gardens, competing well with grasses. The seedpods open in autumn to release beautiful silken, wind-blown parachutes bearing the dark brown seeds. Butterfly weed is completely hardy if the seed source is from a colder region, and does well in any climate but prefers hot summers. Other members of its genus need lots of moisture and are not good candidates for the water-wise garden.

Cultural Information: Prefers infertile, sandy, slightly acidic soils but tolerate almost any. Difficult to transplant except when very young, for it has a long taproot. Late to emerge in spring. Easy to grow from seed. May get some aphids.

Baptisia (bap-TEE-see-a) **wild indigo,** Native American, does well in all but the hottest, driest climates, SP, ESU. ○ ◑

Size: 2 to 5 feet; varies by species
Flower Colors: Blue, white
Water: Best with occasional deep watering.
Characteristics: Wild indigos are graceful, long-lived peren-

nials with cloverlike, blue-green, bushy foliage and loose, erect, 8- to 12-inch spikes of pea-shaped flowers. They are native to the eastern half of the United States, but also grow well in the West. The most waterwise and showy of the group is *B. australis,* wild blue indigo. It is the largest, 3 to 5 feet tall and almost as wide. Its foliage is a beautiful blue-green; the soft blue flowers go well with oriental poppies and peonies, which bloom around the same time. The seedpods dry to an attractive black color. Fully cold-hardy. *B. alba, B. leucantha* and *B. pendula* are a bit shorter, 2 to 4 feet, and have white flowers. *B. pendula* has the added attraction of dark, almost black stems to contrast with the pale blossoms, also lovely with poppies and peonies. The latter two are not quite as hardy as wild blue indigo and *B. alba. B. perfoliata,* Georgia eucalyptus, is not as hardy, tolerating temperatures only to about 0° F. It is grown for its blue-gray foliage, which looks just like flower arrangers' eucalyptus. It grows 2 feet tall and sprawls much wider. The small yellow flowers are not very showy.

Cultural Information: Wild indigos like full sun but will tolerate part shade, where they may become a bit lax and require the help of stakes. They take a few years to reach a sizable clump, but once established are long-lived and drought-tolerant, and dislike being moved. Nick seeds with a knife and then soak in scalding hot water for several hours for best germination.

Baptisia australis

Callirhoe involucrata

Callirhoe involucrata (ka-li-RO-ee in-vo-lu-KRA-ta) **prairie winecup, poppy mallow,** Native American, grows well in any climate, likes heat, LSP, SU, F. ○ ✿

Size: 6 to 12 inches tall, 2 to 3 feet wide
Flower Color: Deep rose, rarely pink
Water: None once established.
Characteristics: Prairie winecup is a long-flowering, sprawling perennial native to the western Great Plains, covering miles of western Kansas and Nebraska like a sea of spilled wine. Palmate, rich, deep green leaves look much like those of hardy cranesbill, as do the 1- to 2-inch cup-shaped flowers. These

have a contrasting white eye. Prairie winecup is semievergreen in mild climates. It combines well with blue flax and silvery plants such as lamb's ear.

Cultural Information: Prefers a sandy soil but will grow in heavy clay, too. Looks the most tidy and compact in poor, infertile soils. If it gets too rangy, it can be cut back hard in mid- to late summer for a new flush of fresh growth. Does not transplant well because of its long taproot. Seeds are sporadic germinators. *C. triangulata* is

Echinacea purpurea

Helictotrichon sempervirens

more upright, up to 3 feet tall, with triangular leaves, but the flowers are almost identical.

Echinacea purpurea

(e-ki-NAY-see-a pur-pu-REE-a) **purple coneflower,** Native American, grows in all climates, SU, LSU. ○ ◑ ▮ ⚡ ✿

Size: 2 to 4 feet tall, 2 feet wide
Flower Colors: Rose pink, white
Water: Occasional deep watering is preferred; needs extra water in hot, dry climates.
Characteristics: Purple coneflower is a robust perennial native to Midwestern prairies. It has coarse, oval foliage and showy, 2- to 4-inch, daisylike flowers. These large blossoms have ray flowers ("petals") that hang down from a stiff, bristly, orange central cone, attracting butterflies and bumblebees. Purple coneflower is not purple at all, but rather a warm rose-pink, and blooms for more than a month in mid- to late summer. 'White Lustre' and 'White Swan' have white flowers, and 'Magnus', 'The King' and 'Bright Star' have more upright "petals." This plant is at home in prairie gardens, with grasses and water-wise species of goldenrods. It is completely hardy. Western plains native *E. angustifolia,* known as black Samson, and southeastern *E. pallida* are not as showy but are plants with significant medicinal uses.
Cultural Information: Does best with some humus incorporated into the soil. Easy to divide and to grow from seed. Deadhead to extend the flowering season. Japanese beetles can be a problem.

Helictotrichon sempervirens

(he-lik-to-TRI-kon sem-per-VY-rens) **blue avena grass,** central Europe, fully hardy, does well in all but the most hot, humid climates, ESU. ○

Size: 2 feet tall and wide
Flower Color: Blue, turning buff with age
Water: Best with occasional deep watering.
Characteristics: Blue avena grass is a lovely, fountain-shaped grass, grown primarily for its steely blue foliage that remains evergreen in all but the coldest climates. The flower is an arching blue panicle rising 1 to 2 feet above the foliage. This grass's form and color make it an excellent foil for just about any flowering perennial, both with hot colors as in the case of orange butterfly weed, and cool pastels such as pale yellow and pink evening primroses.
Cultural Information: Prefers a well-drained soil. Divide in spring. Needs grooming in early spring as the fresh new foliage pushes through and the older begins to turn beige and die.

Lavatera thuringiaca

(la-va-TEE-ra thu-rin-ji-AH-ka) **shrub mallow,** central Europe, good in any climate, hardy to at least −30° F, SU, LSU. ○ ✿

Size: 4 to 6 feet tall, 3 to 4 feet wide
Flower Colors: Rose-pink, white
Water: Best with occasional deep watering.
Characteristics: This large, semiwoody perennial looks like

a shrub yet is best treated as a perennial. Many 2-inch, mallowlike, pink flowers bloom for a month in mid- to late summer, at a time when there is a lull in perennial flowering. The foliage is full, gray-green and lobed. 'Barnsley' is a pretty white cultivar with contrasting rose eyes. Handsome combined with globe thistles (*Echinops*), purple and blue salvias or Russian sage.

Cultural Information: Cut woody stems to the ground each year during the dormant season. Does well in all but the poorest soils. Easy to grow from seed and cuttings. *L. cachemiriana* is taller, up to 8 feet, with less showy flowers.

Limonium (li-MO-ni-um) **sea lavender,** Europe, Central Asia, one from the Canary Islands, grows well in most climates. All except *L. perezii* are hardy to at least −30° F, SU, LSU. ○ ❧ ⚘ ❀

Size: Varies with species
Flower Colors: Lavender, purple, rose, white
Water: Best with occasional deep watering.
Characteristics: Showy, stiff yet airy clouds of tiny, summer-blooming flowers with papery calyces—the outer structure that surrounds the flower—characterize this tough group of perennials. They make excellent dried flowers, like their more well-known relative, the florist's statice. Attractive to butterflies. The foliage is leathery, evergreen and forms a rosette. *L. binervosum* has a 6- to 10-inch-wide, flat foliage rosette of narrow leaves, and 12- to 18-inch stiffly erect, laven-

der flower spikes that age to a warm amber. *L. latifolium* has glossy, large 8- to 10-inch-long, wavy-edged leaves. It blooms in a 2-foot-tall, 3-foot-wide billow of lavender flowers. Cultivar 'Violetta' has larger, showier flowers; 'Robert Butler' is compact at 16 inches; 'Blue Cloud' has pale lavender flowers; 'Collier's Pink' is pink-flowered. All look good with the heavyset daisies of purple coneflower. *L. perezii* is hardy only to about 25° F. The glossy, deep green, lolling foliage is large, up to 1 foot long. Broad, rich purple clusters 2 to 3 feet tall bloom all summer and into fall. *L. (Goniolimon) speciosum* has rose-pink, 2-foot flower clusters. *L. (Goniolimon) tataricum,* Tatarian statice, sends up stiff, prickly, dense, 18-inch clouds of white-calyced flowers over a dark green, 8- to 12-inch wide, flat rosette. Variety *angustifolium* has narrower leaves and pale lavender flowers; var. *nanum* has flowers to only 9 inches.

Cultural Information: Sandy, well-drained, slightly alkaline soil is best. Sea lavenders tolerate wind and seaside conditions. All are easy from seed; sow many, as a large percentage can be sterile. They dislike being transplanted.

Oenothera (ee-NAW-the-ra) **evening primrose, sundrops,** Native American, some highly adaptable to all climates, others less so, LSP, SU, LSU. ○ 🐾 ❀

Size: Varies with species
Flower Colors: White, pink, yellow

Water: Some prefer occasional watering, others prefer none.
Characteristics: This large group of showy plants includes several excellent waterwise perennials, grown for their large, long-blooming, four-petaled flowers, sometimes fragrant. The flowers of some species close during the heat of the day, opening in the evening and on through the night and into morning, attracting moths, while others remain open all day. They tolerate strong wind and thrive in hot summers. All are hardy well below 0° F. *O. speciosa/O. berlandieri*, Mexican evening primrose, ❀ is native to the Southwest and

Lavatera thuringiaca

Limonium binervosum *and* Goniolimon tataricum

Oenothera macrocarpa *and* Oenothera speciosa

Perovskia sp.

Mexico, yet is hardy to about −20° F. It grows 8 to 12 inches tall. In light soil, it can be very invasive, and makes an easy-care, mowable groundcover or planting for a steep bank. 1½-inch, soft pink flowers appear in great numbers in late spring, and on and off until well into fall, remaining open during the day. Foliage is narrow and sparse, deciduous except in the warmest climates. The invasive nature of this plant is not too bothersome, for it is so slender that it peeks up between other plants, rarely crowding them out. Mexican evening primrose responds to occasional watering with more profuse bloom. Vast stretches of it bloom wild in central Texas. *O. caespitosa*, the tufted evening primrose, is a dense mound, 6 to 10 inches tall and a bit wider. Highly fragrant, huge, 3- to 4-foot white flowers with heart-shaped petals open at dusk, and stay open well into the next morning, turning pink as they fade. They are heavily visited by moths. The semievergreen foliage rosettes vary from very hairy and gray-green to smooth and dark green. This evening primrose does well in baked clay soils, thus getting its other common name, gumbo lily. Native to the western Great Plains all the way to California, it requires very dry conditions or else is short-lived. Completely hardy. *O. macrocarpa (missouriensis)* Ozark sundrop, grows almost anywhere but needs occasional deep watering. Huge, 4-inch, fragrant yellow flowers appear sporadically over two months in summer on lax, sprawling, fleshy stems. The plant is 8 to

12 inches tall and twice as wide. The foliage is strap-shaped and fresh green, sometimes tinted red. Large, lime-green, winged fruits are interesting but best removed to promote longer flowering. The flowers close in early afternoon. Ozark sundrop harks from the more eastern Great Plains and Midwest. 'Greencourt Lemon' has paler yellow flowers. Hardy to at least −30° F. *O. brachycarpa* is a smaller, more drought-tolerant version of *O. macrocarpa*, from the Great Plains, sporting 4-inch, yellow, evening-blooming flowers on tidy, dark green, leathery, 6-inch rosettes of foliage. Hardy to at least −30° F. *O. fremontii* is very similar to *O. brachycarpa*, except the foliage is a lovely silver, contrasting well with the huge, pale yellow flowers. Native to Kansas and Nebraska. *O. (Calylophus) hartwegii*, Arizona sundrop, has crinkly, lemon yellow, 1- to 2-inch, late-afternoon- and evening-blooming flowers, almost square in shape, with narrow, hairy leaves on a sprawling, spreading, 6- to 10-inch-tall, 2-foot-wide mat. As the flowers go over, they turn orange. It blooms in spring and summer, and makes a good groundcover. 'Sierra Sundrop' is a longer-flowering selection, hardy to about 0° F. *O./Calylophus lavandulifolia* is similar, with deep yellow, square flowers on a more stiffly shrubby plant, opening in late afternoon and on into late morning the next day, fading to orange. The narrow, gray-green foliage is similar to that of lavender. Native to the western Great Plains.

Completely hardy. *O./Calylophus serrulata* ❀ is a small but profuse-flowering, shrubby 6- to 8-inch evening primrose. The 1-inch, lemon-drop flowers sometimes have a contrasting black eye, and stay open all day. Foliage is narrow and toothed at the edges. It is native throughout the Great Plains and grows well just about anywhere, a highly adaptable, underrated perennial. Completely hardy.
Cultural Information: Easy to grow from seed. Can divide *O. speciosa*. Watch for flea beetles on stressed plants.

Perovskia hybrid (pe-ROV-skee-a) **Russian sage,** central Asia, grows in most climates except where winters are very mild; hardy to at least −30° F, SU, LSU. ○ ❀ ✿.

Size: 3 to 5 feet tall and wide
Flower Color: Lavender-blue
Water: None except in the driest climates.
Characteristics: Russian sage is a shrubby, sagelike perennial with fine, wiry, white stems and tiny, gray-green, pungent, toothed or cut leaves with whitish undersides. Ethereal, hazy blue panicles bloom for six weeks or longer at the end of the summer, gorgeous combined with the pink flowers of shrubby mallow, *Lavatera thuringiaca*. Cultivars of note include 'Blue Haze'; 'Blue Spire' has the most dissected leaves and narrowly upright habit; 'Longen' has larger, deeper purple-blue flowers on a less airy spike.
Cultural Information: Well-drained soil is best. Cut to 6 inches during the dormant pe-

riod each year to promote attractive, vigorous new growth.

Salvia (SAL-vee-a) sage, Europe, Asia, North and South America, prefers hot summers. Hardiness varies greatly. Many with fragrant foliage, LSP, SU, F. ○ ✿

Size: Varies with species

Flower Colors: Purple, blue, lavender, pink, red, white

Water: Some prefer none; most are best with occasional deep watering.

Characteristics: This is an immense group of showy, garden-worthy plants with lipped flowers, often attractive to bees, butterflies and hummingbirds. Many are technically shrubs, but their growth habit and need for a good annual shearing fits them into the perennials category. Their foliage is often aromatic. All have characteristic square stems. Some woodland and tropical sages need a fair amount of moisture to thrive. Generally, they are pest- and disease-free. The following are among the best for waterwise gardens. *S. argentea,* silver sage, is biennial in heavy, cold soils and perennial in well-drained, dry soil. Primarily a foliage plant, it has 6- to 12-inch, large, woolly silver leaves with scalloped edges that loll close to the ground in a rosette. A 3- to 4-foot, loose spike of large white flowers appears in late spring or early summer. Foliage remains more attractive if the flowers are removed. Lovely with pink flowers such as rock soapwort. Silver sage is hardy to at least −30° F. *S. azurea* v. *grandiflora,* blue autumn sage, is a lanky, 4- to 6-

foot-tall, autumn-flowering Midwestern native. The electric blue flowers attract bees and butterflies. A white form exists. The foliage is linear and mid-green, emerging very late in spring. Blue autumn sage is hardy in well-drained soil, needs some extra water for good flowering and looks best when allowed to lean against another plant for support. It is striking against *Rudbeckia triloba,* a tall mass of small, black-eyed Susans, and is pretty sprawling over grasses in prairie and meadow gardens. *S. chamaedryoides,* blue Chihuahuan sage, is a gray-leaved, fine-textured shrublet, 2 feet tall and wide. Azure blue flowers appear all summer and fall in loose spikes. Hardy to about 0° F. Well-drained, dry soil is best. *S. clevelandii,* Cleveland sage, is a shrubby evergreen sage native to California and hardy to 15° F. It grows to a 4- to 6-foot-tall and wide mound with highly aromatic, small, gray foliage. The deep violet-blue flowers bloom in late spring and early summer, in rounded whorls at the tips of the branches. Well-drained soil is a must. Occasional watering prolongs bloom. 'Aromas' has profuse flowers and a compact 3- to 4-foot habit. Prune below old flower clusters after flowering. *S. coccinea,* scarlet Texas sage, is a 1- to 3-foot-tall, Gulf States native hardy only to about 20° F., and grown as a self-sowing annual in the North. Large, 1-inch, red flowers, favored by hummingbirds, bloom from midsummer well into autumn. White and peach forms are

Salvia greggii

available, as are a compact, 1-foot cultivar called 'Lady in Red' and a lovely clear pink, 'Jones' Pink'. Any soil is fine, occasional water is helpful in dry climates. *S. dorrii,* purple desert sage, is a low, 12- to 18-inch, much-branched, shrubby plant with white-felted, small leaves. It is native to the West and hardy to about 0° F., maybe even a bit colder. Showy purple bracts in dense spikes encircle bright lavender flowers in dense heads in late spring and early summer. Purple desert sage likes a very dry soil. *S. farinacea,* mealy-cup sage, 🌿 🔔 is native to Texas. Hardy to about 0° F., it is grown successfully as an annual in the North. 2 to 3 feet tall, it has stiff, navy blue flower spikes that appear from early summer to late fall over glossy, fresh green foliage. Light blue and white cultivars are available. Tolerates most soils; needs occasional water in dry climates. *S. greggii,* cherry sage, is a fine-textured, evergreen, 3-foot, shrubby sage native to the Southwest and Mexico, hardy to about 0° F.

It blooms from spring to fall in typically crimson, 1-inch flowers that attract hummingbirds. Pink, red, orange, white, peach and purple forms are available. The small, rounded, evergreen foliage is rich green and slightly glossy. Well-drained soil is best; little or no water is necessary. *S. leucantha*, Mexican sage, is a tender evergreen shrub, hardy to about 20° F. It has unbranched, arching, 3- to 4-foot stems with white flowers nestled in velvety purple spikes along the top 12 to 18 inches. The gray-green foliage is white underneath, beautifully setting off the richly colored flower spikes. Mexican sage blooms in summer and fall. Cut old stems to the ground in winter. It will tolerate light shade and can go without any water. *S. jurisicii*, from southeastern Europe, is a small, 12- to 18-inch, mounded, deciduous sage with extremely hairy, gray-green leaves, unlike any sage's in that they are finely dissected. The curiously upside-down, lavender flowers bloom on spikes in late spring, superficially resembling catmint. Hardy to at least −30° F. Prefers a dry, well-drained soil. It combines well with dianthus. *S. officinalis*, cooking sage, is a 1- to 2-foot, evergreen, shrubby mound with several lovely foliage selections: 'Icterina', green variegated with yellow; 'Lavandulifolia', larger (3 feet) and shrubby, with narrow gray leaves; 'Purpurea', with dusky plum foliage; and 'Tricolor', the least hardy, with white, magenta and purple marbled foliage. Lavender or white flowers form a loose spike in early summer. Well-drained soil and occasional water are desirable. Hardy to about 0° F., 'Lavandulifolia' to at least −20° F. *S. penstemonoides*, big red sage, is native to the Texas hill country. A shiny rosette of foliage gives rise to 3- to 4-foot flower stems that bloom all summer and fall. The flowers are large and tubular, a rich burgundy color and favored by hummingbirds. Grow as an annual in the North. Tolerates heavier soil than most sages. *S. sclarea* var. *turkestanica* is a perennial form of the beautiful biennial herb, clary sage. It grows 3 to 5 feet tall, with large, hairy, gray-green, 4- to 8-inch leaves and spikes of opalescent white, pink, lavender and rose bracts enclosing small whitish flowers. These bracts remain attractive for two months, from late spring until midsummer. It has a pungent, herbal aroma. It self-sows prolifically. Well-drained soil and occasional watering are ideal. It looks wonderful with pale yellow daylilies such as 'Hyperion'. *S.* × *superba* requires some watering. It has rough, dull-green foliage and long-blooming, tight, indigo spikes from late spring well into summer. Cut it back hard after flowering and it sometimes reblooms. 'East Friesland' is 2 feet tall, great with 'Moonshine' yarrow; 'Mainacht', 18 inches, blooms earlier, lovely with orange, oriental "poppies." There is a rose-flowered cultivar, 'Rose Queen'.

Cultural Information: Most sages are easy to grow from seed and cuttings, and require a well-drained soil.

ADDITIONAL WATERWISE PERENNIALS

Acantholimon spike thrift

Acanthus bear's breech ☾

Achillea yarrow 🐾

Aethionema stonecress 🐾

Agastache giant hyssop 🐾

Agave agave, century plant 🐾

Alcea rugosa yellow hollyhock

Aloe aloe

Alyssum alyssum 🐾

Anchusa azurea alkanet

Anthemis marguerite 🐾

Armeria sea thrift

Artemisia (not *A. lactiflora*) wormwood, silver sage 🐾

Aspidistra elatior cast-iron plant ☾

Aster divaricatus ☾

Aster ericoides heath aster

Aster × *frikartii* Frikart's aster

Aster linearifolius

Aster sericeus silky aster

Astragalus pea vetch

Aubrieta purple rock cress

Aurinia saxatilis basket-of-gold

Ballota

Bergenia pigsqueak ☾

Berlandiera lyrata chocolate flower 🐢

Bouchea linifolia

Brunnera macrophylla Siberian forget-me-not ☾

Calamagrostis × *acutiflora* 'Stricta' feather reed grass

Calamintha nepetoides calamint 🐾

Catananche caerulea Cupid's dart

Centaurea knapweed

Centranthus ruber Greek valerian W

Cephalaria yellow pincushion flower

Chrysopsis golden aster

Convolvulus (some)

Coreopsis

Cortaderia selloana pampas grass

Corydalis lutea yellow fumitory ☾ 🐾

Coryphantha cactus

Crambe sea kale 🐾

Cynoglossum hound's tongue ☾

Dasylirion sotol, desert spoon

Deschampsia caespitosa tufted hair grass ◐

Dianthus (not *D. barbatus*) pinks 🐢

Diascia twinspur

Dictamnus albus gas plant 🐢

Digitalis lanata Grecian foxglove

Dorycnium hirsutum

Dracocephalum dragon's head 🐢

Dudleya

Echeveria hen and chickens

Echinocereus hedgehog cactus

Echinops globe thistle

Erianthus ravennae ravenna grass, hardy pampas grass

Eriogonum buckwheat (see groundcover portrait, p. 82) 🐢

Eriophyllum woolly sunflower, golden yarrow

Erodium stork's bill

Eryngium sea holly

Erysimum wallflower 🐢

Eupatorium rugosum white snakeroot ◐

Euphorbia spurge (some) W

Evolvulus

Ferocactus barrel cactus

Ferula ferula 🐢

Festuca fescue

Filipendula hexapetala dropwort 🐢

Foeniculum vulgare 'Purpureum' bronze fennel W 🐢

Gaillardia × *grandiflora* Indian blanket

Galega officinalis goat's rue

Gaura apple blossom grass

Geranium (small rock-garden spp.) cranesbill

Gutierrezia sarothrae broom weed

Gypsophila baby's breath

Helichrysum licorice plant, curry, strawflower 🐢

Heliopsis helianthoides summer sun

Hemerocallis daylily ◐ 🐢

Hesperaloe red yucca

Heuchera sanguinea coral bells ◐

Hieracium hawkweed W

Hypericum St. John's wort ◐

Hyssopus officinalis hyssop 🐢

Iberis sempervirens candytuft ◐

Incarvillea olgae tall hardy gloxinia

Ipomoea leptophylla bush morning glory

Iris —arilbred hybrids, bearded iris 🐢

Iris douglasiana hybrids Pacific Coast hybrids

Iris spuria (*I. orientalis*) spuria iris

Knautia macedonica ruby pincushion flower

Kniphofia red hot poker

Koeleria cristata June grass

Lavandula lavender 🐢

Leonotis leonurus lion's tail

Liatris aspera, *L. punctata*, *L. spicata* gayfeather

Linaria toadflax W

Linum flax

Lithospermum canescens, *L. caroliniense* puccoon

Lithospermum incisum

Lupinus lupine (most) 🐢

Lychnis coronaria rose campion

Malva mallow

Mammillaria pincushion cactus

Marrubium horehound

Melampodium leucanthum Blackfoot daisy

Mirabilis multiflora desert four o'clock

Neobesseya cactus

Nepeta catmint 🐢

Nierembergia hippomanica cup flower

Nolina beargrass

Ononis

Onosma 🐢

Opuntia prickly pear, beaver tail, cholla cactus

Origanum showy oregano 🐢

Oryzopsis hymenoides Indian rice grass

Oxytropis locoweed

Paeonia peony 🐢

Panicum virgatum switch grass

Papaver poppy

Pediocactus snowball cactus

Pennisetum setaceum fountain grass W

Penstemon beardtongue

Petalostemon prairie clover

Petrorhagia (*Tunica*) *saxifraga* tunic flower

Phlomis Jerusalem sage 🐢

Phygelius cape figwort

Potentilla hippiana horse potentilla

Psilostrophe paper flower

Pulsatilla pasqueflower ◐

Ratibida prairie coneflower

Romneya tree poppy 🐢

Ruellia wild petunia

Ruta graveolens rue 🐢

Sansevieria snake plant ◐ 🐢

Santolina lavender cotton 🐢

Scabiosa pincushion flower 🐢

Schizachyrium scoparium little bluestem

Schrankia sensitive briar 🐢

Sedum stonecrop 🐢

Sempervivum hen and chickens

Senecio cineraria dusty miller

Sidalcea malviflora checkerbloom

Sideritis

Silene laciniata Indian pink

Solidago goldenrod (some)

Sorghastrum nutans Indian grass

Sphaeralcea cowboy's delight, desert mallow

Stachys lamb's ear, betony (see groundcover portrait, page 83)

Stanleya prince's plume

Stillingia texana

Stipa comata needle and thread grass

Symphytum comfrey ◐

Tagetes lemmonii bush marigold 🐢

Tagetes lucida sweet-scented marigold 🐢

Cerastium tomentosum

Eriogonum umbellatum

Talinum fame flower

Tanacetum densum v. *amani* partridge feather

Teucrium germander 🐾

Verbena bonariensis Buenos Aires vervain W

Verbena stricta Plains vervain 🐾

Veronica incana silver speedwell

Veronica spicata spike speedwell

Viguiera showy goldeneye

Viola (some) violet ◐ 🐾

Xerophyllum beargrass, turkeybeard 🐾 ◐

Yucca Spanish bayonet, soapweed, datil 🐾

Zauschneria hummingbird's trumpet

Zinnia grandiflora desert zinnia

Five Waterwise Groundcovers

The following plants are all perennial, but what differentiates them from those mentioned previously is that each forms a dense carpet, either spreading underground or on the soil surface. Foliage takes on a vital role; many of these plants have showy flowers, but attractive leaves for much of the year are prerequisite for consideration as an effective groundcover. There are many uses for these plants aside from the more obvious berm covering or shrub and tree underplanting. Those with less aggressive habits and root systems serve as excellent companions to bulbs, framing the bulbs' flowers with foliage and hiding their shabby leaves as they die back to the ground. Consider growing two or more groundcovers of similar growth rate and cultural needs together to form a patchwork.

Cerastium tomentosum (se-RAS-tee-um to-men-TO-sum) **snow-in-summer**, Mediterranean, grows in any climate except very hot, humid ones. Completely hardy, LSP, ESU. ○ ◐

Size: 6 to 10 inches tall, unlimited spread

Flower Color: White

Water: Little to none once established; a fuller, more rampant groundcover with occasional watering.

Characteristics: Snow-in-summer is a pretty, dainty-looking perennial whose appearance belies its highly aggressive ways. It spreads by thin underground runners. Narrow oval to linear, dense, semievergreen, silver foliage spills prostrate across the ground. Above this hovers a pure white, snowy haze of small, starry flowers for several weeks in late spring and early summer. Good for banks and slopes, also between shrubs and paving stones. Pretty when combined with the equally aggressive Mexican evening primrose, *Oenothera speciosa* (page 77). The two duke it out and form an intertwined carpet of pink, white and silver. Cultivars 'Yo-Yo' and 'Silver Carpet', and variety *columnae* are all more compact, 3 to 6 inches tall. *Cerastium bierbersteinii* is very similar, with a somewhat less rambunctious habit and larger flowers.

Cultural Information: Tolerates any well-drained soil, and spreads fastest in sandy soils. Shear back to almost half its height after flowering to promote thick, bushy, attractive foliage, otherwise it gets straggly. Easy to divide.

Eriogonum umbellatum (e-ri-AH-go-num um-be-LAY-tum) **sulphur flower,** Native American, completely hardy; suffers in hot, humid climates, LSP, SU. ○ ◐ ❀ 🐱 🏃

Size: 6 to 12 inches tall, 10 to 18 inches wide

Flower Color: Yellow

Water: Little to none once established.

Characteristics: This evergreen, western American native is really a small shrub; it is widespreading and self-sowing, making a good groundcover. The oval, 1-inch foliage is borne in rosettelike clusters and varies from deep, slightly glossy, leathery green to quite silver on top; the undersides are always felted white. Showy, profuse, sulfur yellow puffballs, technically compound umbels, bloom and then turn a rusty bronze as they dry and set seed, lengthening their ornamental period well into late summer. Fall and winter foliage color is an attractive reddish brown or burgundy. Good on slopes to control erosion; deerproof. Many beautiful, long-blooming, shrubby California natives exist but have very limited use outside that region. Two good for groundcover use there are: *E. grande rubescens*—similar to the sulphur flower but with rosy red flowers; and *E. fasciculatum*, California buckwheat, a 1- to 3-foot-tall-and-wide groundcover with gray-green foliage and creamy pink flowers; 'Theodore Payne' is an excellent, shorter, greener cultivar. These species are hardy only to about 20° F.

Cultural Information: Buckwheats need a well-drained

soil. They take windy and seaside conditions. Easily grown from seed.

Stachys byzantina (STAH-kis bi-zan-TEE-na) **lamb's ears,** Near East, hardy to at least −40° F.; grows in all climates except the most hot and humid, ESU. ○ ◑ ⚘

Size: 4 to 8 inches tall without flowers (18 inches with), 1 to 2 feet wide
Flower Color: Lavender-pink, not showy
Water: Little needed once established; avoid overhead watering.
Characteristics: This groundcover is a favorite of children for its soft, silvery, woolly foliage. The leaves are narrowly oval, 2 to 6 inches long, evergreen in mild climates, and lie flat on prostrate, semiwoody stems. The insignificant flowers are hidden in 18-inch, woolly, silver spikes that are pretty in dried arrangements. These give an interesting shape and texture to a planting. After flowering, the tired foliage takes a month or so to grow back. Nonblooming cultivars exist: 'Silver Carpet', and the larger, less silvery 'Helene von Stein'. 'Primrose Heron' has chartreuse-yellow foliage in early spring, turning to gray by midsummer; 'Sheila McQueen' is a compact form. 'Cotton Ball' has dense, bobblelike flower clusters. Many other attractive, water-wise species of *Stachys* exist, but are not good for groundcover. Lamb's ears looks great with most plants; try it with sea lavender or prairie winecup.
Cultural Information: Good drainage is best. Lamb's ears tolerates seaside conditions,

high winds and intense, but not muggy, heat. Remove spent flower stalks promptly to help foliage come back. Needs dividing and replanting every few years to keep at its freshest and fullest. After a cold, wet winter, remove much of the saggy, old foliage to make room for new.

Verbena (ver-BEE-na) **verbena, vervain,** North and South America, does well in any climate with sufficiently hot summers. Cold hardiness varies with species. Some have fragrant flowers, LSP, SU, F. ○ ⚘

Size: Varies with species
Flower Colors: Lavender, pink, rose, purple, red, white
Water: Some fine with none, others best with occasional deep watering.
Characteristics: Verbenas include several sprawling plants that make good groundcovers. Showy clusters of flowers bloom for many months and are attractive to butterflies and occasionally hummingbirds. They are an excellent choice for hillsides and are fire-retardant. Their foliage is evergreen in warm climates. The lovely flowers are enhanced in combination with silver artemisias or lamb's ears. Most species self-sow. *V. bipinnatifida*, prairie verbena or Dakota vervain, is a Great Plains native and hardy to at least −40° F. It grows 6 to 12 inches tall and 2 to 3 feet wide. Clusters of lavender or violet-pink flowers bloom from spring until late autumn. Lush green, deeply cut foliage clothes the sprawling stems. These stems root along as they go, making a denser ground-

cover. Prairie verbena gets by with no additional irrigation. Excellent in shortgrass prairie gardens. *V. canadensis* is very similar, with flowers a bit larger and more fragrant; it is not as reliably hardy a plant in spite of its name; hardier seed may change this in the future. 'Gene Cline' is low-growing with deep rose flowers; 'Candidissima', white; 'Glowing Violet', 'Lavender' and 'Rosea' are colored as their names suggest. *V. gooddingii* is native to the Southwest and hardy to about 10° F. It grows up to 18 inches tall and twice as wide. The pale lavender flower clusters are fragrant, rising above a hairy, green mound of cut foliage. Southwestern verbena prefers sandy soils and needs no supplemental water, but blooms longer if given some. *V. peruviana* is a South American perennial, hardy to about 25° F. and grown as an annual in colder climates. It does best with occasional deep watering. The fine-textured, airy, 6-foot-tall, 2- to 4-foot-wide mat of evergreen foliage is dotted with brilliant red clusters in the species; pink, rose, white and purple cultivars are available. *V. rigida*, tuberous verbena, is a showy purple-flowered, upright, 1- to 2-foot plant that is frighteningly invasive and rapidly becoming a roadside weed in the South. 'Alba' has white flowers; 'Polaris', also sold as 'Lilacena', has icy lavender blooms. It works well as an annual in cold-winter climates. Hybrid 'Flame' has scarlet flowers and is only 6 inches tall. *V. tenera* is almost exactly like *V. peruviana* except a

Stachys byzantina

Verbena tenera *and* Verbena tenuisecta

bright shrimp pink. 'Albiflora' has white flowers; var. *maonettii* has rose flowers edged with white. *V. (Glandularia) tenuisecta*, moss verbena, is perennial to 15° F. and can otherwise be grown as an annual. It is fine-textured and demure in stature—6 to 10 inches tall and twice as wide. Fresh green, ferny, evergreen foliage is studded with dainty clusters of bright lavender. Can be mowed to 3 inches after the first flush of bloom for neatness. 'Alba' has white flowers; 'Edith' is pink.
Cultural Information: Verbenas do best in heat, with good air circulation. They tolerate any well-drained soil, seaside conditions and strong wind. Overhead watering may cause mildew in humid climates. They do not like being moved or divided, but grow well from seed or cuttings.

Veronica liwanensis

Veronica (ve-RO-ni-ka) **speedwell**, Asia Minor, completely hardy, grows in all but the hottest, most humid climates, ESP, SP, ESU. ○ ◑

Size: Varies with species
Flower Colors: Blue, pink, white
Water: Best with occasional deep watering.
Characteristics: There are many wonderful perennial veronicas, most requiring regular watering. The following two are drought-tolerant and make excellent groundcovers. They are both evergreen and low-growing, forming an attractive mat. *V. liwanensis*, Turkish veronica, is the more refined of the two, growing a bit more slowly and completely prostrate. The tiny, glossy, rounded leaves make an excellent cover for small spring

bulbs such as crocus and snow iris. In late spring, Turkish veronica bursts into several weeks of breathtaking blue bloom. The individual flowers are tiny, with white eyes. *V. pectinata*, woolly speedwell, is a bit more robust and aggressive. The toothed, woolly, gray-green foliage forms a dense, 4- to 6-inch mat, taking on purplish tints in the winter. It blooms in early spring, with sporadic rebloom throughout the year. Lovely with pale yellow, dwarf bearded irises. 'Alba' and 'Rosea' are white- and pink-flowered cultivars.
Cultural Information: Well-drained soil is best. Easy to divide.

ADDITIONAL WATER-WISE GROUNDCOVERS

(See also lawn alternatives, page 23–25)

Acacia redolens 'Prostrata' acacia ☀

Achillea tomentosa woolly yarrow (see page 25) ☀

Aizoaceae iceplant family *Aptenia, Carpobrotus, Cephalophyllum, Delosperma, Drosanthemum, Lampranthus, Maleophora, Mesembryanthemum* and others

Anacyclus depressus Mt. Atlas daisy

Antennaria pussytoes (see page 25)

Arabis rock cress ☀

Arctostaphylos manzanita ◑

Arctotheca calendula capeweed

Artemisia wormwood, silver sage ☀

Aspidistra elatior cast-iron plant ◑

Baccharis sarothroides 'Centennial' desert broom

Campanula poscharskyana creeping bellflower ◑

Ceanothus (prostrate forms) California lilac ☀

Ceratostigma plumbaginoides dwarf plumbago ◑

Cistus salviifolius sageleaf rockrose (see shrub portrait, page 72) ☀

Convolulus sabatius (C. mauritanicus) ground morning glory

Coronilla varia crown vetch W ☀

Correa pulchella Australian fuchsia ☀

Cotula squalida brass buttons ◑

Crucianella (Phuopsis) stylosa crosswort ◑

Cytisus broom W ☀

Dalea greggii trailing indigo bush ☀

Duchesnea indica Indian strawberry ◑ W

Elymus blue lyme grass, dune grass W

Epimedium barrenwort ◑

Erigeron karvinskianus profusion daisy W

Euphorbia robbiae Miss Robb's spurge ◑ W

Galium odoratum sweet woodruff ◑ ☀

Gazania rigens var. *leucolaena* trailing gazania

Genista broom W ☀

Geranium macrorrhizum creeping cranesbill ◑ ☀

Glechoma hederacea ground ivy ◑ W ☀

Hedera helix English ivy ◑

Helianthemum nummularium sun rose

Hemerocallis daylily ◑ ☀

Hypericum St. John's wort ◑

Juniperus juniper ☀

Lamiastrum galeobdolon yellow archangel ◑ W

Lamium maculatum deadnettle ◑

Lantana lantana W ☀

Liriope spicata lilyturf ◑ W

Nepeta catmint ☀

Oenothera speciosa Mexican evening primrose (see perennial portrait, page 77)

Origanum vulgare 'Aureum' golden oregano ◑ 🐛

Osteospermum barberae, O. fruticosum freeway daisy

Paronychia pearlwort

Pentzia incana karroo bush

Persicaria (Polygonum) affinis Himalayan fleece flower ◑

Phlox bifida, P. douglasii, P. subulata moss phlox 🐛

Potentilla nevadensis creeping potentilla

Pterocephalus creeping pincushion flower

Rhus aromatica 'Gro-low' fragrant sumac (see shrub portrait, page 66) 🐛

Rosmarinus officinalis (prostrate cultivars) rosemary 🐛

Rudbeckia fulgida var. *sullivantii* 'Goldsturm' black-eyed Susan

Rumex scutatus creeping sorrel ◑

Santolina lavender cotton 🐛

Saponaria ocymoides rock soapwort

Scutellaria skullcap

Sedum stonecrop (some for ◑) 🐛

Silene vulgaris ssp. *maritima* sea campion, maiden's tears

Symphytum grandiflorum yellow comfrey ◑

Teucrium chamaedrys 'Prostratum' prostrate germander 🐛

Thymus thyme 🐛

Vancouveria hexandra Vancouver fern ◑

Vinca minor periwinkle ◑

Viola (some) ◑ 🐛

Waldsteinia barren strawberry ◑

Zauschneria hummingbird's trumpet

WATERWISE ANNUALS AND BIENNIALS

The following plants bloom either the first season (annuals) or second season (biennials) from seed and then die. Some so-called annuals are perennial in the mildest climates, but don't overwinter successfully in most regions and for that reason included here. The plants highlighted here are, of course, water-wise. Ease of care plus a tendency to self-sow and reappear reliably year after year without requiring gardener intervention also figured strongly in the following selection. Another quality these 8 annuals and biennials have in common is a "perennial look"; many annuals, especially the highly bred and hybridized favorites, are not only not water-wise but also don't mix well with other plants. Their flower color, size and shape are so domineering and overbearing that they overshadow all their companions. By contrast, the following plants have all the good qualities of annuals—easy to grow, long-blooming and floriferous—and yet are good mixers, socializing well with both shrubs and perennials, and with each other.

Consolida ambigua

(kon-SO-li-da am-BI-gwa) **larkspur,** Mediterranean, best in cool weather, LSP, SU. ○ ◑ 🍶 🌿 ✿

Size: 3 to 5 feet

Flower Colors: Indigo, blue, pink, rose, white

Water: Occasional deep watering.

Characteristics: Annual larkspur is an old-fashioned cottage garden plant that mixes well with perennials. It serves as an easy-care substitute for stately yet fussy delphinium spires. It is very cold-tolerant, making foliage growth early in the season. Bright green, ferny leaves give rise to stiff yet delicate flower spikes for two months of bloom before the hottest days of summer set in. Flowers are 1 inch across, single or, more commonly, double. Larkspur makes a wonderful cut flower and also dries well, keeping its color. The flowers attract butterflies and hummingbirds. The common deep blue form is wonderful with the warm gold of perennial coreopsis; try the pastels with silver-leaved, brilliant magenta rose campion, *Lychnis coronaria.*

Cultural Information: Best in infertile, well-drained soil with little water; otherwise, needs staking. Larkspur needs cool temperatures to prepare for germination and dislikes transplanting. Sow seeds in fall or winter where they are to grow and cover them with ⅛ inch of soil for better germination. Plant in light shade in hot-summer regions, or mulch the roots. Self-sows dependably. Deep blue forms will dominate over pastel forms in the self-sown population over time.

Cosmos bipinnatus (KOZ-mos by-pi-NAY-tus) **garden cosmos,** Mexico, grows anywhere, likes summer heat, SU, F. ○ ✿ 🍶

Size: 2 to 6 feet tall and wide

Flower Colors: Pink, crimson, white

Consolida ambigua

Cosmos bipinnatus 'Sensation'

Dyssodia tenuiloba
'Golden Fleece'

Nigella damascena

Water: Occasional deep watering in dry climates.

Characteristics: Large, 2- to 6-inch daisies over a lush bushy mass of ferny, fresh green foliage have made this annual so popular. The species doesn't bloom until late summer and autumn, when the days begin to shorten. Better cultivars with large, early flowering blooms are the 'Sensation' series, including crimson 'Dazzler', and rose 'Radiance' with a red eye. Double forms with ruffled centers include 'Double Crested', 'Psyche' and 'Anemone-Flowered'. 'Sea Shells' has rolled, spoon-shaped ray flowers, the "petals"; 'Daydawn' is white with a rose eye; 'Purity' is pure white. The compact, 2-foot 'Sonata' series is excellent and easier to combine with other plants in the garden. Try it with purple-flowered Mexican sage or the indigo spires of mealycup sage (pages 79 and 80). Cosmos's long, slim stems make it a great cut flower. Self-sows dependably. This semitender annual tolerates light frost and seaside conditions but will blow over in strong wind. It attracts butterflies. *C. parviflorus,* southwestern cosmos, ✿ is native and shorter at 2- to 3-feet tall. Pale pink, 1-inch

flowers float over sparse foliage in late summer and fall. *C. sulphureus* ✿ is earlier-flowering and shorter, with smaller, 2-inch flowers in bright shades of yellow, orange and orange-red. The foliage is less finely cut and darker green. It often flowers itself to a premature demise, going completely to seed by late summer. Birds fancy the seeds. 'Lemon Twist' is a good 2- to 3-foot-tall yellow-flowered form; 'Diablo' is 4 feet with brilliant orange-red flowers. 'Sunny Gold' and 'Sunny Red' are two compact, 12- to 16-inch, semi-double cultivars.

Cultural Information: Infertile, well-drained soil is best, or the plants grow too much foliage at the expense of flowers and tend to fall over. Deadheading greatly prolongs the flower display. Simple and fast from seed; can be sown in place or started beforehand. Excellent plant for children to grow. Needs warmth to germinate and grow.

Dyssodia (Thymophylla) tenuiloba (di-SO-dee-a te-nu-i-LO-ba) **Dahlberg daisy,** Texas and Mexico, does well in all climates, ESU, SU, F. ○ ✿

Size: 4 to 10 inches tall, 8 to 10 inches wide

Flower Color: Yellow

Water: None, once established, except in the driest climates.

Characteristics: Dahlberg daisy is a pretty, fine-textured annual, covering itself with little, ½- to 1-inch, yellow daisies. The finely cut, green foliage sets these off perfectly. Sometimes it will self-sow. Dahlberg daisy makes an excellent edging plant or annual groundcover. It is sometimes called golden

fleece. Several nasty-smelling, sometimes prickly relatives (called "dogweeds" for a reason) are native to the Southwest; be sure to procure only *D. tenuiloba.* Dahlberg daisy is a semitender annual and can tolerate light frost. It may act as a short-lived perennial in the warmest climates.

Cultural Information: Prefers a sandy soil but will grow in any well-drained soil. Easy to start from seed.

Eschscholzia (e-SHOL-zee-a) **California poppy,** Native American, best where nights are cool, SP, SU, F. ○ ✿

Size: 6 to 18 inches tall, 12 inches wide

Flower Colors: Orange, gold, yellow, red, purple, crimson, rose, cream

Water: None, once germinated and growing well; occasional in the driest climates.

Characteristics: California poppies, also copa de oro (cup of gold in Spanish), paint much of the California hillsides brilliant, golden orange in spring—a good choice for the state flower. They are perennial to 10° F., annual elsewhere. Four large, satiny petals form a cuplike flower, 1 to 3 inches across. These have a light, spicy fragrance and close at night, not opening until the sun is well up in the sky the next morning, giving them their other Spanish common name, *dormidera*—sleepy one. Lovely blue-green, finely cut, smooth foliage works as the perfect foil for the showy flowers. Self-sown seedlings are a given if the long, slender seedpods are allowed to form. In very mild winters, California poppies may begin flowering as early as February. They tolerate seaside conditions and wind. Lovely combined with blue flax or deeper blue desert bluebells, *Phacelia campanularia*. Cultivars include: 'Cherry Ripe', crimson; 'Double Monarch' and 'Mission Bells', double, all colors; 'Ballerina' and 'Thai Silk', all colors with semidouble fluted and fringed petals; 'Milky White'; 'Purple-Violet'; and 'Dalli', single scarlet flowers with yellow centers. *E. mexicana* is similar but a bit smaller, with bluer foliage, and deeper orange flowers. It is even more drought- and heat-tolerant. *E. caespitosa*, also called bridal bouquet, is smaller—4 to 10 inches—and more dainty, with yellow flowers and tufted, sparse foliage. 'Sundew' has fragrant, lemon yellow flowers. *E. lobbii* is similar.

Cultural Information: Any infertile, well-drained soil will do. Deadheading after the first big flush of bloom helps prolong flowering through the heat of summer. Sow directly in place in the garden; California poppies hate transplanting. The seeds need a period of moisture and then cool temperatures to germinate, so fall sowing is best in areas with mild, moist winters; sow in early spring elsewhere.

Nigella damascena (ny-JE-la da-ma-SEE-na) **love-in-a-mist, devil-in-the-bush,** Mediterranean, best in cool weather, SP, ESU, SU. ○

◑ ⚘ ▮

Size: 1 to 2 feet tall, 4 to 6 inches wide
Flower Colors: Blue, lavender, rose, pink, white

Water: None, except in the driest climates.
Characteristics: This delicate-appearing yet tough, frost-hardy annual has ferny, green foliage on stiff, narrow stems. Love-in-a-mist blooms early in the season, before it becomes too hot; in cool-summer regions, it can be sown again in early summer for late-summer and fall bloom. The rounded, many petaled, 1- to 2-inch flowers are also encased in a ferny froth, hence the common name. They are highly popular with bees. Papery, inflated, oval, 1- to 2-inch seedpods with a crown of hornlike bracts gave rise to the devil allusion. These pods are excellent in dried arrangments; the flowers are good cut fresh. Love-in-a-mist self-sows like there's no tomorrow. Pretty when threading through bearded iris, with bright pink dianthus or *Silene armeria*. Good cultivars include: 'Miss Jekyll', a pure, sky blue; 'Miss Jekyll Alba', white; 'Persian Jewels', mixed colors; and 'Mulberry Rose'. *N. hispanica* is very similar but a bit taller; its flowers are slightly larger, lavender-blue with orange anthers and a black eye.
Cultural Information: Needs good drainage. Remove seedpods before ripe if you don't want a forest of self-sown seedlings. Sow where to grow in fall or early spring; love-in-a-mist resents transplanting.

Phacelia campanularia (fa-SEE-lee-a kam-pa-nu-LA-ree-a) **desert bluebell,** Native American, best with cool nights, SP, SU. ○ ◑ ✾

Size: 6 to 18 inches tall and wide

Eschscholzia californica

Flower Color: Deep blue
Water: Occasional watering in dry climates prolongs bloom.
Characteristics: This California desert native blooms after early spring rains in the wild, before the intensely hot season. 1-inch, rounded, toothed leaves are covered with reddish hairs, as are the semitrailing stems. Beware when handling this plant—the hairs can cause a rash in sensitive people, and the sap stains hands and clothes brown. ½- to 1-inch, bell-shaped flowers in loose clusters are a deep gentian blue, sometimes visited by hummingbirds. Desert bluebells are hardy, tolerating light frost. They self-sow in light soils. Combine them with California poppy or Dahlberg daisy for a brilliant color display.
Cultural Information: Needs a well-drained, preferably somewhat sandy soil. Sow seed in place in fall or early spring and don't cover; desert bluebell dislikes transplanting and needs light to germinate.

Phacelia campanularia

Silene armeria

Silene armeria (sy-LEE-ne ar-ME-ree-a) **annual catchfly, none-so-pretty,** Mediterra-

nean, grows in any climate, SP, SU. ○ ◐

Size: 12 to 18 inches tall, 6 to 12 inches wide

Flower Colors: Bright pink, rarely white

Water: None, except in the driest climates.

Characteristics: This annual has waxy, blue-green, oval leaves in a rosette from which arise several upright stems topped with 3- to 5-inch clusters of brilliant pink flowers. None-so-pretty blooms for about two months and may act as a biennial in mild climates, growing a rosette in the fall from seed of that spring and summer's flowers. It self-sows and has naturalized in parts of this country. It is often included in annual meadow mixes with blue bachelor's buttons and red corn poppies. Cultivars are 'Electra' and 'Royal Electric', especially profusely flowering; and 'Alba', with white flowers. Nice when combined with love-in-a-mist, blue flax or the blue and pink flowers of viper's bugloss or borage.

Cultural Information: Any well-drained soil will do.

Verbascum (ver-BAS-kum)

mullein, Europe, Mediterranean, Asia Minor, completely hardy, will grow well except where summers are very hot and humid, ESU, SU. ○ ✿

Size: Varies with species

Flower Colors: Yellow, white, pink, purple

Water: Little to none, once established, except in the driest climates.

Characteristics: Mulleins are stately biennials and perennials. They are very promiscuous, hybridizing freely with one an-

Verbascum bombyciferum

other. Typically, a tall flower spike rises from an attractive rosette of large leaves. The perennial species can tolerate light shade, do not bloom as long and need a bit more water. These include *Verbascum chaixii,* 2 to 4 feet with gray-green leaves, yellow or white flowers; Cotswold hybrids, 3 to 4 feet, pink, yellow, peach, buff or white flowers; *V. phoeniceum,* 2 to 3 feet, with green leaves and white, pink, wine or purple flowers. The following are the best biennial mulleins for water-wise gardens: *V. blattaria,* moth mullein, has dark green, smooth leaves and grows 4 to 5 feet tall. Seek out the lovely white-flowered form with contrasting purple anthers. *V. bombyciferum* has a woolly, white, 2-foot foliage rosette from which rises a 4- to 6-foot spike, also densely white-felted, with 1-inch, lemon-yellow flowers for more than two months in summer. 'Arctic Summer' is especially showy and felted. *V. densiflorum/-thapsiforme* has large green leaves covered with tawny hairs. The flowers are the largest of the mulleins, 2 inches across, on 5- to 6-foot, branched spikes for two months. *V. olympicum* is the giant of the lot, with a 6- to 8-foot, branched, bright yellow candelabrum of flowers over a gray, felted, 2- to 3-foot foliage rosette. *V. undulatum* stays about 2 feet tall, with narrow spikes of small yellow flowers. The foliage is fantastic—long leaves with ruffled, undulating margins, covered in bright yellow felt as though dusted with sulfur. *V. wiedemannianum* is an elegant newcomer, 3 to 4 feet tall, with gray leaves and a

flower stalk of beautiful 1-inch, purple flowers. It is the most difficult to grow.

Cultural Information: Verbascums grow easily from seed. Well-drained soil is necessary. Watch for spider mites in hot climates.

ADDITIONAL WATERWISE ANNUALS AND BIENNIALS

B: may be biennial
P: may be perennial in warmer regions
W: may be weedy in some regions

Cool Weather: These plants do best in cool weather, or at least cool nights; get them planted either in fall in mild climates or as early as possible in the spring in cold-winter/hot-summer climates. They provide winter color in the hottest regions. Most can tolerate a light frost.

Ammi majus laceflower
Arctotis African daisy
Brachycome iberidifolia Swan River daisy 🐢
Calandrinia rock purslane P 🐢
Calendula officinalis pot marigold 🐢
Centaurea cyanus bachelor's button
Cheiranthus allionii Siberian wallflower B 🐢
Clarkia satin flower
Crepis rubra hawksbeard
Daucus carota Queen Anne's lace B W
Diascia twin spur P
Dimorphotheca cape marigold P
Dorotheanthus bellidiformis Livingstone daisy
Echium lycopsis viper's bugloss B
Felicia blue marguerite P

Gilia capitata thimble flower

Gypsophila elegans annual baby's breath

Iberis annual candytuft 🐢

Lathyrus odoratus sweet pea 🐢

Layia tidytips 🐢

Linum annual flax

Mesembryanthemum crystallinum iceplant

Nama demissa nama

Nemophila fivespot, baby blue eyes

Osteospermum African daisy P

Papaver poppy B

Phlox drummondii annual phlox 🐢

Trachymene coerulea blue laceflower

Venidium fastuosum cape daisy

Warm Weather: These plants thrive in summer's heat and won't grow well without it. Most should not be planted out into the garden until the weather is reliably warm.

Argemone prickly poppy B P

Catharanthus roseus Madagascar periwinkle P, ◖

Eriogonum annuum white buckwheat

Gaillardia pulchella annual Indian blanket

Gomphrena globosa globe amaranth

Helianthus annuus sunflower

Ipomopsis rubra standing cypress B

Kallstroemia grandiflora desert poppy

Kochia scoparia var. *trichophylla* burning bush W

Lantana P W 🐢

Melampodium leucanthum Blackfoot daisy P

Mirabilis jalapa four-o'clock P 🐢

Monarda citriodora lemon beebalm, horsemint B 🐢

Oenothera evening primrose P (see perennial portrait, page 77) 🐢

Perilla frutescens beefsteak plant W

Portulaca grandiflora moss rose

Psilostrophe paper flower P

Salvia sage P (see perennial portrait, page 79) 🐢

Tagetes marigold P 🐢

Talinum fameflower P

Tithonia rotundifolia Mexican sunflower, torch flower

Verbena P (see groundcover portrait, page 83) 🐢

Verbesina encelioides crownbeard

Viguiera annua golden eye

Zinnia angustifolia narrow-leaf zinnia

Zinnia haageana Mexican zinnia

Warm or Cool Weather: These plants are not as particular regarding temperature and will do well in both cool and hot climates.
F: tolerates light frost

Abronia/Tripterocalyx sand verbena P 🐢

Alcea rosea hollyhock B P F

Antirrhinum majus snapdragon P F

Atriplex hortensis 'Rubra' red orach F W

Baileya multiradiata desert marigold B P F

Borago officinalis borage F

Cleome bee plant, spider flower

Coreopsis P F

Cynoglossum amabile hound's tongue B F

Dianthus chinensis pinks P F 🐢

Emilia javanica tassel flower

Erigeron karvinskianus profusion daisy P F W

Euphorbia marginata snow-on-the-mountain F

Foeniculum vulgare 'Purpureum' bronze fennel P F W 🐢

Gazania treasure flower P

Glaucium horned poppy B F

Hedysarum coronarium French honeysuckle P F 🐢

Helichrysum petiolatum licorice plant P 🐢

Humulus japonicus hops vine P PS F W

Hunnemannia fumariifolia Mexican poppy B F

Ipomopsis aggregata skyrocket gilia B

Lavatera trimestris annual mallow

Limonium sinuatum statice B

Linaria maroccana toadflax F

Lobularia maritima sweet alyssum F 🐢

Lupinus lupine F 🐢

Machaeranthera Tahoka daisy B F

Matthiola bicornis evening stock F W 🐢

Mentzelia blazing star B F 🐢

Nierembergia hippomanica cup flower P

Nolana paradoxa blue trumpet P

Onopordum Scottish thistle B F W

Orthocarpus purpurascens owl's clover, escobita

Pennisetum fountain grass P F W

Rhynchelytrum repens ruby grass P W

Rudbeckia hirta black-eyed Susan P F

Salvia farinacea mealy-cup sage P F (see perennial portrait, page 79)

Salvia sclarea clary sage B P F (see perennial portrait, page 80). 🐢

Sanvitalia procumbens creeping zinnia

Senecio cineraria dusty miller P F

Silybum marianum milk thistle B F W

Thelesperma greenthread P F

Tropaeolum majus nasturtium F 🐢

Xeranthemum annuum immortelle

PESTS AND DISEASES

Plants, like all other living things, are subject to pests and disease. If you practice good waterwise gardening—choosing plants well-adapted to your climate and garden conditions, watering them deeply but only when necessary and maintaining them as needed—your plants will be healthier. The less stress a living being undergoes, the better it is able to fight off illness. Pests and disease-causing organisms attack the most weakened, compromised plants available to them. In conventional gardens, often these are plants that depend on a lot of water and don't get it. Sometimes it is just the opposite; overwatered and overfertilized plants, lush, soft and floppy, attract pests, while hardened, tough growth remains relatively unscathed.

Another way to keep your garden healthy is to grow many different kinds of plants. A greater variety of plants supports a greater variety of creatures, including beneficial predators that will help keep potential pests in check. Also, if one particular species in a diversified garden succumbs, it is less noticeable than if that same species exists as a monoculture, such as an acre of grub-infested, blighted lawn or a 30-foot berm of rodent-girdled junipers.

SELECTIVE WARFARE

By growing the right plant in the right place, we minimize potential problems. However, even the healthiest garden suffers from occasional outbreaks. As with watering, we need to change our ways of handling this. Just as we shouldn't water until the plants require it, we shouldn't apply chemicals on a predetermined basis according to some rigid calendar. Instead, we need to control pests and disease only once we're certain the plants need our intervention. By blindly applying pesticides and fungicides, we endanger the environment, including ourselves. Insects and disease organisms have built up resistance to the overused chemicals, and useful predators have been decimated. The ecosystem's balance, both in the garden and beyond, has been disrupted and damaged.

Be more vigilant. This way you can catch a problem before it gets out of hand. If you see the first few aphids of spring clinging to a young rosebud, you can remove them by hand rather than having to spray the whole bush. It is vital that you identify the offending pest or disease and its plant victim. If you can't do this with the help of a good book, have your county extension agent or an expert at a nursery or botanical garden assist you. You need to know the enemy before you can fight it. You may be blaming an innocent bystander, or worse, a helpful predator, for the damage. Next, determine whether the interloper is really a problem and worth the effort. Is the damage it causes serious enough to warrant intervention? We have developed a zero-tolerance attitude toward pests and diseases, while ironically fostering a highly tolerant attitude toward the use of potentially dangerous chemicals. A few holes in a leaf are really not so terrible.

If you decide your intervention is needed, try several approaches before you resort to chemicals. You can pick off and squish many insects. A sharp spray of the hose will dislodge many an aphid and mite. A fire-blighted branch can be pruned out. Traps, baits and lures will catch a number of interlopers, both mammal and insect; barriers will keep them away. Seek the help of predators and biological controls, which are becoming more available and diverse all the time. As a last resort, consider the least toxic chemical controls. These include horticultural-grade oils, soaps, insect growth regulators and dusts and sprays from botanical sources such as sabadilla, rotenone, pyrethrum and neem. These substances are not completely harmless, but they break down quickly and leave no toxic residues. Read the label, follow instructions and apply only where actually needed—to the affected area.

Once you have accomplished this, assess how best to avoid the problem arising again. Introducing predators will help. You may want to change certain conditions and practices that have favored the outbreak of the problem. For example, watering in early morning rather than at night will help if you are having fungal problems on plant foliage. Let the garden dry out thoroughly between watering and keep it relatively free of dead plant material to reduce earwigs, pillbugs, sow-

bugs and slugs. If the problem keeps recurring in spite of your efforts, consider removing the affected plant and replacing it with a more resistant variety or trying another species altogether. If you can't part with the plant, move it to another location in the garden with different conditions; perhaps it will be healthier and happier there. There are so many garden-worthy plants out there—both newer, tougher forms of old favorites as well as novel species. Experimentation breeds success.

ENLIST HELP

Invite insectivorous birds such as robins, house wrens, starlings, blue jays and northern flickers into your garden with enticing habitats—shrubby areas, a birdbath and large conifers for cover and roosting. Add appropriately built and sited birdhouses to encourage nesting. If you are really lucky, you may host an owl in a large

old tree. Don't forget the less appealing helpers, the creepy-crawlers we love as children but grow to dislike and fear as adults, including such nice guys as snakes, toads and spiders. Learn to identify the beneficial insects from the potentially troublesome ones; curb your impulse to squash anything that crawls. Ladybug

larvae, assassin and pirate bugs and ground and rove beetles, though not as attractive as butterflies, are valuable allies in the garden.

Now for a look at some specific pests and diseases. Each region has its indigenous and introduced problems. The ones listed here may occur in a broad range of waterwise gardens.

FUNGAL DISEASES

Fungal diseases trouble waterwise gardens much less than conventional gardens. Texas root rot and oak root fungus can be kept at bay by planting resistant species and avoiding frequent, shallow waterings. If you have areas of poor drainage (which are susceptible to root rot), build raised beds or install drainage tile. Downy mildew, leaf spot, botrytis, rust and black spot thrive in moist conditions and can be minimized

by avoiding overhead watering and providing adequate sunshine and air circulation. Remove all infected plant parts from the garden. Powdery mildew is the least harmful of the lot, but thrives in seemingly arid conditions. Either live with it or spray potentially afflicted plants with an antitranspirant, fungicidal soap, summer oil or a weekly spraying of a 0.5 percent solution of baking soda and water (3 teaspoons per gal-

lon) before the gray film covers more than just a few leaves. Adding 2½ tablespoons of 0.5 horticultural spray oil or soap to the baking soda solution helps it adhere to the foliage, making it more effective. It is species-specific, so although it may look like the same disease is afflicting both your roses and lilacs, they are actually distinct and can't spread from one type of plant to another.

BACTERIAL DISEASES

There is little you can do against these diseases except select resistant plants and keep them as healthy as possible through proper culture. The biggest bacterial problem in waterwise gardens is fireblight, an often fatal infection that afflicts many woody members of the rose family. It is most prevalent in the hot-summer/cold-winter climates of the Midwest, Great Plains and Rocky Mountain regions. Prune infected, scalded-looking parts to unafflicted wood; disinfect your pruners or saw between each cut with 70 percent rubbing alcohol, a 20 percent bleach-and-water solution or Lysol. Some plants are able to fend off an infection, losing small twigs every summer but never deeper down a branch. Others get one infection and the whole plant is killed in a season. Moist conditions and too much fertilization increase a plant's chance of infection.

SLUGS AND SNAILS

Slug

These slimy nocturnal creatures thrive in cool, moist, dark places. A sunny garden, allowed to dry out well between waterings, is rarely plagued by slugs or snails. Good housekeeping—removing plant debris and loose pots, stones, bricks and sundry objects under which the offenders like to hide—is also important. Put barriers of diatomaceous earth or copper strips around susceptible plants and make use of baits of stale beer or a solution of sugar water and yeast. If you have a resident toad or two, take heart; they are great slug and snail eaters. Drip or soaker-hose irrigation is better than overhead watering in deterring the outbreak of slugs and snails. Rotting fruit and citrus rinds attract them and can be used to catch a large number.

SPIDER MITES

These tiny relatives of spiders and ticks prefer the exact opposite conditions of slugs and snails—sunny, hot and dry. For this reason they are probably the most widespread problem in waterwise gardens. They are hard to identify before they have caused significant damage, for they are only the size of finely ground pepper and do their work on the undersides of leaves, usually on the lower, older foliage of a plant. An afflicted leaf will seem webby and dusty beneath and bronzed, dry and sometimes almost burned-looking on top. Spider mites usually attack plants that are not as well adapted to intense heat or dry conditions, such as spruces native to cool mountains and temperate-zone members of the rose family. Often plants subjected to the intense heat and lack of air circulation found close to a wall will succumb before the same plants do out in the garden. Daily dousing with a strong spray of water will discourage spider mites but not get rid of them altogether. Diligent, repeated applications of soaps are more effective for severe infestations. Oil sprays during the dormant season will control eggs. If mites keep coming back to haunt you, perhaps you need to rethink your palette of plants.

Snail

Spider mite

EARWIGS

Red spider mite

Contrary to folk wisdom, these unattractive, elongated brown insects will not climb in your ear and eat your brains. The frightful rear-end pinchers are harmless. However, these nocturnal feeders may ruin flowers by feeding on the petals. If the problem gets out of hand, you can trap them by providing favorite hiding places during the day such as moist newspaper or a wooden board. Insecticidal baits are also available. Earwigs have positive attributes, too. They eat aphids and insect larvae, and have the endearing quality of being one of the only insects that looks after its young. Think of the mother earwigs nurturing their youngsters next time you recoil upon meeting up with one.

APHIDS

Aphids are very common. It is highly unlikely that you will go through more than a season or two as an avid, observant gardener without encountering a few. These small, slow, soft, teardrop-shaped insects suck the juice from moist, young, often overfed plant parts. By themselves they cannot kill a plant, though in sufficient numbers they can stunt new growth and cause malformations. However, they should be kept under control for they spread much more serious, incurable viral diseases. Outbreaks are common in spring when plants have much succulent new growth not yet hardened off to the weather, or after a dose of too much high-nitrogen fertilizer. They come in winged and wingless forms, green, red, gray, black or yellow, and like spider mites, reproduce at a prodigious rate. You are most likely to find them under young leaves or clinging to new buds, stems and shoots. They secrete a sticky honeydew, which may also help you identify the problem. You can remove them by hand, with a strong spray of water, or by using insecticidal soaps or neem. All these strategies need to be repeated several times to wipe them out. Trap crops—easily grown plants highly attractive to the pests, such as nasturtium and calendula—can be planted to concentrate them in a small area, making control easier. Several natural predators help: ladybug larvae, aptly named aphid monsters; lacewings; and tiny parasitic wasps.

Aphids

BEETLES, WEEVILS, GRUBS AND BORERS

These are difficult pests to control, for the larvae usually bury themselves underground or within plants, out of the reach of all but the most toxic controls, and the adults are often nocturnal or can come from great distances. Biological controls appear to be the most promising tactic. These are expensive and take time to work, but are effective. Milky spore disease is being used against Japanese beetles, applied to grub-infested lawns. Handpicking these metallic, sex-crazed beetles in the morning while sleeping on their plant victims will help somewhat, but there are always more coming from yonder. Lures help the gardener capture and kill remarkable numbers, but many come not to the trap itself, only to its vicinity, so you may find beetle damage in your garden increases after you put up a lure. Other strains of species-specific bacterial diseases and parasitic nematodes are proving effective against black vine weevils and several species of leaf beetles and borers. Hopefully their more widespread use will help curb these damaging insects.

Beetle

Japanese beetle

THRIPS

Thrips are tiny tan or silver insects that damage the flowers of many plants, especially introduced and intensely hybridized species. They are most troublesome in warm, mild climates. Thrips are notoriously hard to control because they hide within the folded petals of flowers and inside developing buds. If exposed, they can be dispatched by overhead watering and insecticidal soaps. Light blue sticky paper works well as a trap for the flying adults. Remove infested blossoms from the garden and burn.

GRASSHOPPERS

Grasshoppers are a problem in arid regions, especially in less urban areas. They are fast, ravenous and not picky about what plant they eat. These insects have cyclical outbreaks just as the Bible suggests. The newest and most promising control is biological, a species-specific parasitic protozoan called *Nosema locustae.* It takes several applications and some time to work, but is proving quite effective in grasshopper-afflicted areas if applied early enough when the grasshoppers are still young and more susceptible. Birds prey on grasshoppers, as do some cats, but the latter may flatten your garden in pursuit. Free-roaming poultry have been used for control.

WHITEFLIES

Whiteflies are tiny white insects that have a characteristic erratic way of flying, often in great clouds around an infested plant. You can vacuum them while they hover. They are attracted to yellow sticky paper traps. Insecticidal soaps, neem and oil sprays are effective in killing the nonflying, immature forms, usually found on the undersides of leaves. Regular, repeated applications are necessary for adequate control. Lacewings eat them.

Whiteflies

CATERPILLARS

Caterpillars turn into moths or butterflies: Ravaging hornworms become fascinating sphinx and hawk moths; the large striped parsleyworm grows into the beautiful black swallowtail butterfly. For the most damaging types, either hand-pick them or apply *Bacillus thuringiensis* spray against susceptible species such as hornworms and tent caterpillars. The latter are easily removed as a group encased in their webby nest or burned in place with a torch. Caterpillars have many natural enemies, including birds, toads, parasitic wasps, ants and assassin, soldier, stink and pirate bugs. Neem and oil sprays are also effective.

SCALES AND MEALYBUGS

These slow-moving insects are soft inside, protected by an outer shell or fuzzy coating. They gather in leaf and stem axils, under leaves and along stems. Dormant oil sprays work against the adults, summer-oil and insecticidal soap applications can be timed to hit the unprotected, immature crawlers. Small infestations can be controlled by removing the pests with an alcohol-dipped cotton swab. Birds eat some scale insects.

MAMMALS

You may become quite unpopular if you let nongardeners know you are out to control adorable rabbits, chipmunks, squirrels and innocent-eyed deer. Most gardeners will be sympathetic, however. Various rodents can cause a great deal of damage to plants, digging up and eating bulbs, girdling plants by chewing their bark, and munching on new shoots and flowers. Traps with appropriately enticing baits will catch many rodents, but most of us don't want to go to the trouble of transporting the prisoners for distant release, or worse yet, have to execute them ourselves. This chore is preferably left to cats, who will kill mice, voles and chipmunks and deter larger rabbits and squirrels, sometimes preying on them as well. However, cats will also kill insectivorous birds, so the news is not all good. Hot pepper sauce mixed with anti-transpirants and sprayed on susceptible plants works as a taste repellent. Burying wire mesh just above bulb plantings keeps out digging rodents. Be sure to keep mulch away from the trunks of trees to prevent nesting and girdling.

Deer are notoriously serious garden pests. Dogs deter most mammals, including deer, but are not compatible with gardens if allowed to roam freely. An 8-foot wire mesh fence will keep out deer, as will a 5-foot electric fence with charged wires at 8- to 12-inch spacings. Strategically placed dog and cat scat, and regular applications of commercial repellents, help keep deer at bay.

Please write or call for a free Burpee catalog:

W. Atlee Burpee & Company
300 Park Avenue
Warminster, PA 18974
215-674-9633

Index

Prentice Hall and the W. Atlee Burpee Company
are pleased to extend to readers of the
Burpee American Gardening Series these special offers:

Burpee American Gardening Series Readers:
Save $3.00
with This Exclusive Offer!

There are lots of good reasons why thousands of gardeners order their seeds, bulbs, plants and other gardening supplies from the Burpee Gardens Catalogue: highest quality products, informed and courteous service, and a guarantee on which you can depend.

Now there's another good reason: you can save $3.00 on an order of $10.00 or more from the 1994 Burpee Gardens Catalogue. This is an exclusive offer available only to readers of the Burpee American Gardening Series. Just enclose this coupon with your order and deduct $3.00 from the total where indicated on the order form from your catalogue.

If you need a Catalogue just send in the coupon below.

Your signature _____

This discount coupon must accompany your order. **Offer expires 12/31/94.**

This offer is not transferable. No photocopies or facsimiles of the coupon will be accepted. Coupon has no cash value and may not be redeemed for cash or exchanged for products at retail stores. Offer void where prohibited, taxed or otherwise restricted.

FREE!
Gardening's Most Wanted Catalogue!

Start your garden or expand it with high quality products from Burpee. The 1994 Burpee Gardens Catalogue features seeds, bulbs and plants for new varieties of flowers and vegetables as well as hundreds of old favorites and a broad range of garden supplies. Send in this coupon today to:

W. Atlee Burpee & Company
000646 Burpee Building
Warminster, PA   18974

Please send me a free 1994 Burpee Gardens Catalogue.

Name _____

Street _____

City _____ State _____ Zip _____

Cut along dotted line.

000646